THE SONG OF SONGS
The Greatest Love Song

Exploring the mystery of love in courtship and marriage

MATTHEW H. VANLUIK

xulon
PRESS

The Song of Songs
The Greatest Love Song
by Matthew H. VanLuik

Printed in the United States of America.

ISBN 9781498426169

Scripture quotations taken from the The Holy Bible, New International Version (NIV). Copyright © 1973, 1978, 1984, 2011 by Biblica, Inc.™. Used by permission. All rights reserved.

www.xulonpress.com

To my wife Gertie

Table of Contents

Foreword

$\mathcal{I}$t is not always easy in our current sensual, sex-saturated, neo-pagan, hedonistic culture for Christians, young or old, to fully appreciate the true meaning of love, sex and marriage as intended by the Creator. As a result there is a great need for resources that can give a biblical, countercultural view of what God had in mind when he created the first human male and female and officiated at their wedding as he presented Eve to Adam.

Rev. Matthew VanLuik has succeeded admirably in giving such a resource by turning to God's Word, specifically to the Song of Songs, a book too often neglected or misunderstood by well-meaning Christians. In his clear and sound exposition of this part of Scripture, he unpacks the beautiful and encouraging message found in these love poems, which are at the same time God's Word for the instruction of his people. With pastoral sensitivity Rev. VanLuik shows the meaning of true love, the gift of our sexual identities and the precious institution that is marriage. The author is fully aware of the challenges of our sinful nature and the current culture. He is sympathetic to the needs, pitfalls and frustrations of staying pure in an unholy world and understands that Christian marriages are not always what they should be because of sin. Over against these concerns, the message of this book is full of practical wisdom and hope. Rev. VanLuik gives biblically based direction and encouragement for all aspects of love, courtship and marriage.

This book is an excellent resource for young people for developing a positive view of sex and embarking on a loving relationship with that special person. Questions addressed include premarital sex, what to look for in a future wife or husband and how to prepare for marriage. Married couples will also benefit from the biblical wisdom offered here in developing a healthy and joyous lifelong loving relationship with each other in honouring their respective God-given roles. Reading and studying this book will also enable one to see ever more clearly how our courtships and marriages are to reflect something of the love that Christ, the great bridegroom, has for his bride, the church.

A valuable feature of this book is the concluding section of each chapter which invites further reflection with questions for discussion. Such a conversation can take place within the family circle or in a Bible study group. In this way topics that can be quite sensitive can be more easily openly discussed in an edifying manner. Then we can encourage each other in opposing the corrosive culture of our times and building biblical attitudes and foundations for lifelong blessings.

Read and study the biblical wisdom of this book and do not forget the helpful introductory chapter. May the Lord be pleased to use this exposition and application of his Word for his glory and for the well-being of his people.

Cornelis Van Dam

Acknowledgements

With deep gratitude I thank my dear wife, Gertie, for her loving support. During thirty-five years of marriage I have often reflected how fortunate I have been for her constant support and care, even when on many occasions I became preoccupied with the work of ministry. This work can become all-consuming and therefore it is a blessing to have a life companion who is not only patient but also keeps my feet firmly planted in reality. Working on the Song of Songs has been a rich blessing for our relationship, as I was constantly reminded by the Spirit not only of the joys of marriage but also the responsibilities that come with it. Because we love so imperfectly, the Spirit's constant encouragement is so important.

I also thank my wonderful daughter, Lorraine, for her constant encouragement and interest in this work. Her questions about the song and her insight into human relationships were always helpful and above all stimulating. The Lord has now blessed her with a supportive husband, Neil, and given them a beautiful daughter who gives great delight to her grandparents.

The Lord also brought into our life Erin Tenhage-Kampen, who became like a second daughter to us. Erin spent many hours reading through the manuscript and providing valuable feedback. Since then she has become married to her great love, Nick. I also thank Nick for using his talents in designing the cover for this book.

I am grateful to my congregation for their support and to the elders of the church for their encouragement to publish this work on the song. I thank the congregation for the valuable time they gave me to begin the initial writing of this work. Without the constant support of many this work would not have become a reality.

My thanks also to Dr. Cornelis Van Dam for graciously reading the manuscript and providing valuable insights. I very much appreciated his helpful suggestions for maintaining a consistent approach to the interpretation of the song.

I also benefited greatly from the editing work of Julie van Tol, who was willing to fit this into her busy schedule. It was her challenge to ensure that I both wrote in a logical way and maintained a consistency in style. The art of communication is to effectively convey thoughts and ideas for the reader. Where this book fails to communicate as effectively as it should is not the fault of the editor but the fault fully rests with me. I am grateful to Kirsten Sloots for preparing the document for publication by doing the copy edit.

Although mentioned last, yet of first importance is the care and blessing of the Lord, who has made this work possible. In my work on this song I have come to better understand God's loving care for his people through the redeeming work of his Son, Jesus Christ. This song celebrates the saving work of the Lord and reminds us of his love and faithfulness for his people. That blessing is priceless.

Introduction

What to expect from this book

The Song of Songs has a history of controversy. Today there is general agreement that this song belongs to God's Word, but there is still much controversy about its meaning and purpose. I took on the challenge of preaching on this song in response to questions from young couples. They asked questions about the meaning of the song: what is its message for us today and why is there so much sensual language in it? I do not claim to have the last word on the interpretation of this song, but I hope that this work will add something to the ongoing discussion and answer some of these questions. It was gratifying to receive positive feedback from young and old alike as they listened to an exposition of this portion of scripture that for many of them had seemed like a closed book.

It should be clear that this book is not intended as an exegetical work, but it is rather an attempt to help readers to better appreciate a part of God's Word which has often been overlooked, and apply it to their lives in a practical way. I have attempted to do so first by understanding the song within the context of the ancient reader (as much as that is still possible) and then by conveying its practical application for the New Testament church.

The goal of this work is to understand more fully what the text reveals about God's work for his people and how that needs to be applied in our life of service to God. We will need to reflect on what the text teaches about our relationship first with God and then how that should be reflected in our relationships with others and especially in our marriages. We will be asking such questions as: what does the song teach us about our own characters or the character that we should pursue for our own life as people of God? For example, in the first two chapters of this book the woman gives a description both of the man she loves and of herself (1:2–8), allowing us to consider their characters and how certain aspects of their characters are important to a relationship. From this it will become clear what kinds of character we need to develop in our own lives as we pursue a relationship. There will also be occasions when I will draw from pastoral experience to talk about some real concerns and struggles couples face in their relationships.

My prayer is that this book may be used by the Spirit to help the reader grow in his or her love and commitment to a gracious God and that this love may be the basis on which husbands and wives grow in their love and commitment for one another. I have tried to avoid many of the technical discussions and arguments found in the commentaries. When I felt that I should make the reader aware of other arguments or additional details, I have placed that information in a note. Since I began this study, a number of excellent commentaries have been published on this song, and they should be consulted for a more in-depth exegetical study of the book.

Love songs

Love has been an enduring theme persisting through every age and in every culture. Love songs tend to be among the most popular songs, romance novels still capture people's fascination, and movies often have a romantic love interest to maintain the viewers' attention. Love is a common topic of conversation that is surrounded with an air of mystery since it is difficult to understand why a certain man is attracted to a certain woman, and vice versa. How does one explain the mystery of a man and woman desiring to live together in marriage for the rest of their lives? Who can understand why a man will bound over mountains and cross oceans in order to win a woman's heart?

God created human beings with the need to love and to be loved. One of the first stories in Genesis tells us that the first man, Adam, felt alone, and the Lord said it was not good for a man to be alone. Therefore, God created the woman, Eve, from the rib of the man and he gave her to Adam. Then Adam responded with the first love song:

> "This is now bone of my bones
> and flesh of my flesh;
> she shall be called 'woman,'
> for she was taken out of man."
> (Genesis 2:23)

Not long after this, Adam and Eve rebelled against God by eating fruit from the forbidden tree (Genesis 3). Their rebellious attitude not only affected their relationship with God, but it immediately affected their own relationship when Adam blamed Eve for his disobedient action against God. Sin distorted the human understanding of love and frustration entered into the marriage relationship. Sin has the power to skew our understanding about love with the result that we no longer fully grasp the great mystery of the loving bond between a husband and wife. The Lord gave the Song of Songs to help us begin to understand and learn to celebrate his beautiful gift of love again.

To understand the love experienced by the couple in this song, we first need to understand and experience God's love for his people. In the scriptures, the Lord often speaks about his relationship with his people in terms of a marriage. On many occasions in the Old Testament, the Lord accuses his people Israel of committing spiritual adultery by becoming unfaithful to him. The New Testament teaches that Jesus Christ is the great bridegroom and that the church is his bride, called to live in a faithful and committed relationship with him (Ephesians 5:21–33). From a biblical perspective, it can be argued that the marriage relationship reflects something of our relationship with Christ or, I think it is better to say, our relationship with Christ should be reflected in our marriage relationship. Therefore, we will need to explore what the Song of Songs reveals about Christ's love for his people. In the same way that Christ shows his love for us, husbands ought to love their wives, and just as the church is called to love Christ, wives are to love their husbands. This is the mystery we need to explore in the Song of Songs in order to fully understand its significance and meaning for marriage.

Why a love song?

In the history of both the Old and New Testament church, believers have often felt uncomfortable with this love song, and yet the opening words declare that it is the "Song of Songs." This is a typical Hebrew method of expressing a superlative thought, similar to such expressions as "Lord of lords" or "Holy of Holies." The Holy of Holies is the most holy place in the temple; the Lord of lords is the greatest of all rulers. Therefore "Song of Songs" conveys that this is the greatest and the most beautiful song, exceeding all the songs in the world.

Around 100 AD, the Jewish rabbi Aqiba disputed an opinion held among some Jewish scholars that this song had no authoritative status in the Bible. They questioned whether this song should even be considered as part of the Old Testament scriptures. Aqiba wrote, "No man in Israel ever disputed about the Song of Songs ... for all the ages are not worth the day on which the Song of Songs was given to Israel; for all the Writings are holy, but the Song of Songs is the Holy of Holies." In his estimation, the day that Israel received this song was to be considered the greatest day in Israel. The fact that this song is considered to be the greatest of all songs is a surprising commendation for a song that makes many people uncomfortable with its sensual content. But if this is indeed the greatest of all songs, as scripture also attests, then we cannot ignore it. We may be thankful that God speaks so openly and frankly about the relationship between two people who are in love with each other.

So why does the Lord include such a love song in his Holy Word? The Song of Songs is, in fact, one of a small group of books of the Old Testament referred to as wisdom literature.[1] In these books, we find wise and practical instruction for the ordinary things of daily living. God imparts such wisdom so that his people may develop the necessary skills for their daily lives. Since marriage is one of the more important life events, it should not be a surprise that the

Lord includes a book like the Song of Songs in the Bible in order to instruct us about courtship and marriage. The song is not a step-by-step instruction manual, however, but gives snapshots of the courtship and marriage of a man and a woman who express their love for each other poetically, while at the same time revealing something of the mystery of marriage. As the couple expresses their love for each other, they also expose the cares, concerns and difficulties that come with such a relationship. Love is beautiful, but it also involves challenges. There is a great need for the wisdom found in this song because we have lost any understanding of genuine love and true passion, due to our sinful nature. People no longer understand what God intended for marriage relationships, with the result that today we live in a sexualized society offering a very jaded and corrupt view of our sexuality.

As mentioned, this love song is not a how-to manual that gives a number of steps that will help to improve your relationship. Instead, in the song we follow the courtship of a couple whose love for each other grows in a very natural way, and who display a tender care and longing that they have only for each other. They are completely devoted to one another. That is the way the Lord intended marriage to be in the very beginning, and how he wants his people to experience and enjoy marriage today. The faithful love between a husband and wife is to be celebrated, because it gives great joy and a wonderful stability. Because it speaks about love between spouses as God intended it to be, this song is called the greatest of all songs. Adam rejoiced when the Lord gave Eve to him as his wife (Genesis 2:23), because the Lord had given him a companion and she was exclusively his. The Lord gave him a woman with whom he could share the deepest thoughts of love, who was truly one with him and with whom he could commune with his whole heart. That is what the Lord intended for marriage. This song is the most excellent song for it reveals the wonderful mystery of love between a man and a woman.

The identity of this couple

The man in the song is often identified with Solomon since Solomon's name is mentioned seven times in the song. The man is never actually referred to as Solomon, however, and in every case where Solomon's name is mentioned it is used for the purpose of comparison (Song of Songs 1:4, 5, 12; 3:9, 11; 7:5; 8:11, 12). For example, in 1:5 the girl compares her dark complexion to the curtains of Solomon's tent, and in chapter 3 Solomon's name is used three times in a description of his glorious wedding procession. It may be argued that these references show that this woman had some connection with Solomon, but Solomon's name is never used in any context where the couple speaks intimately to one another. Rather, his name and reputation usually offer a contrast to some aspect of the couple's life. In chapter 8:11–12, we have an example of this, when the couple declares that Solomon may have many riches but what they have is much better and more glorious than anything Solomon has.

It is also difficult to support the theory that it is Solomon who declares his love for the woman of this song. She is a common farm girl who works in her parents' vineyard and takes care of their young goats. And when the woman looks for the man she loves in 1:7–8, she describes him as a shepherd, a description that does not fit the situation in Solomon's life. His father David had been a shepherd when he was a young man, but not Solomon. This man and woman both come from the same social background, growing up in the country and accustomed to working on a farm and looking after the sheep and vineyards. It is difficult to imagine that Solomon is expressing love for a girl of a much lower social standing in his kingdom.

There is no evidence in the song to help us determine a specific identity for the couple. If the song is composed of a collection of poems, as is likely (wisdom literature is usually composed of a collection of sayings or poems), that would make it impossible to identify them with any particular couple. Therefore, it may be best to understand this song as an expression of the love between an anonymous or even fictional Israelite couple[2] given as an example of the love that should be reflected in the life of every couple in Israel.

If the man in the song is not Solomon, then is he perhaps the author of the song? The song's opening words, "Solomon's Song of Songs," have led to the commonly held opinion that Solomon is the author, an assumption that has increasingly come into question. The Hebrew text of the opening words is not helpful in settling the question of authorship, for the little connecting word in this phrase can mean either that it is a song "of" Solomon or "for" Solomon. Translated as "of" Solomon, it suggests that Solomon wrote the song, but translated as "for" Solomon it means that the song was either written for Solomon's own benefit or dedicated to him. Therefore, Solomon's authorship cannot be determined from the title itself.

As a support for the case of Solomon's authorship, one could argue that since the Bible speaks about Solomon's great wisdom, surpassing all other wisdom in the whole world, therefore Solomon might have had the skill to write the greatest of all love songs. But love and marriage are areas in his life for which the scriptures do not commend Solomon. 1 Kings 11 says that Solomon loved many foreign women; he married Egyptian, Moabite, Ammonite, Edomite, Sidonian and Hittite women. The Lord explicitly says that Solomon sinned when he married women from foreign nations: "'You must not intermarry with them, because they will surely turn your hearts after their gods.' Nevertheless, Solomon held fast to them in love" (1 Kings 11:2). In addition to these wives, he had seven hundred other wives and three hundred concubines, and on account of these wives and concubines, scripture says that Solomon was led astray. Solomon clearly showed no wisdom when it came to matters of the heart. While many of his marriages were the result of political alliances, the scriptures tell us that these women captured Solomon's heart so that he turned to other gods.

Since Solomon is mentioned in the song, however, we can conclude that the song likely came into existence in the period after his reign. It is later, during the reign of King Hezekiah, that we read about the collection of wisdom literature (Proverbs 25:1). The Song of Songs is part of this wisdom literature, a genre which typically includes collections of writings; for example, the book of Proverbs is a collection of wisdom sayings from various authors over a long period of time. Within the wisdom genre, it would be natural that this song is a collection of love songs written by various authors. Keel suggests that since Solomon was famous for his many relationships with women, it would not be surprising that anonymous Israelite love songs of all kinds, over time, were increasingly ascribed to Solomon as the great patron of both love and songs (39).

If we indeed have a collection of love songs from different sources in Israel, the author's purpose for this reference to Solomon in the opening words seems to be to contrast Solomon's approach to love relationships with the kind of love God really intended for marriage. As one commentator puts it, "Solomon is a foil for this author's broader purposes" (Provan 235). As a foil, Solomon's own relationship with women represents the antithesis or exact opposite of what a proper or godly relationship between a man and woman should be. In this scenario, it is possible that the title of this song is used to set up a contrast with Solomon. It already implies at the outset that the audience should not think about love in the way that Solomon did, for it only led him astray. There is a better and a much more beautiful and glorious way. That better way is the love that is expressed by this man and woman for one another.

Structure and composition of the song

The song's structure is very orderly, and its content is divided around a refrain found in 2:7, 3:5 and 8:4, "Daughters of Jerusalem, I charge you by the gazelles and by the does of the field: Do not arouse or awaken love until it so desires." Each section builds up to the refrain, after which there is an abrupt scene change. In each section, the author directs the focus of the reader to another aspect in the life of this couple, suggesting the following division of the song:

1. 1:1 — Introduction
2. 1:2–2:7 — Love awakens
3. 2:8–3:5 — Love blossoms
4. 3:6–8:4 — Love and marriage
   a. 3:6–5:1 — The wedding day
   b. 5:2–6:9 — Challenges in marriage
   c. 6:10–8:4 — Joys in marriage
5. 8:5–14 — Living in the security of love

With this approach, the song becomes, or can be read as, a collection of love poems that the author has edited into one song. Rather than a life story of a couple in Israel, the poems touch on stages of their relationship. Beginning with poems that describe the awakening of love in the lives of a young couple, the song then moves on to describe the deepening of their love and the couple's desire for marriage. As he moves through the stages of life, the author incorporates poems describing the marriage feast, the consummation of the marriage and then the ongoing challenges in marriage itself. All of these themes are skilfully woven together to form a complete representation of the joys and difficulties that every couple will experience in their relationship.

The Song of Songs within the context of scripture

To grasp the significance of this love song, it needs to be understood within the overarching biblical story. In the beginning, God gave Eve to Adam and she became his wife. At first they enjoyed a beautiful marriage relationship in which love functioned as God intended, but the love they had for each other became distorted after they sinned against God. With this song, God reveals that he has restored the possibility of a loving marriage relationship for his people if they again submit themselves to his will.

I maintain throughout this book that this love song can only be properly understood through the saving work of Jesus Christ. The Lord Jesus came to save the world and restore everything that was broken by sin. One of the very first things that broke after Adam and Eve sinned was their marriage relationship. Instead of declaring his love for Eve and taking responsibility for his sin, Adam accused Eve of causing him to sin. He said to God in Genesis 3:12, "The woman you put here with me—she gave me some fruit from the tree, and I ate it." The bond between them was broken and the true song of love was no longer heard in paradise. The Lord saw what was happening in the garden and how sin affected the relationship between Adam and Eve. For that reason, the Lord promised to give Eve a child who would save them from their sins. God fulfilled that promise by sending his own Son, and Jesus Christ in his great love gave his life for his people. It is on the basis of Christ's love that mankind can again love God and their neighbour. Christ's love is the basis on which husbands and wives can again truly love each other in a sacrificial way.

In the Old Testament setting of this song the people did not yet know Jesus Christ, but they believed in God's promise concerning the Saviour, the promised offspring of Eve. On the basis of that promise, the believers in Israel could already begin to experience in their relationships the love this song celebrates. Men and women of faith who have been redeemed by the blood of Christ and experience God's loving grace, can again sing this most excellent song of love. When a man and woman share the love that this song reveals, they will experience great joy. Those who sing this song together in Christ will find contentment and peace in their relationship.

Historical interpretations

Historically, the Christian church has approached this love song with a sense of uneasiness because of the sensual nature of its subject matter. In it, the man and woman speak openly to each other about their love, and they are not afraid to express their physical longing for one another. In the past, attempts have been made by the church to soften the song's sensual language. After all, the Lord also makes very clear that we are to keep our bodies pure with regard to sexual matters. But at the same time, the Lord gave this song that explicitly speaks about the strong yearning this couple experiences, resulting in a tension that we may find difficult to bridge.

To deal with this tension, attempts have been made to downplay the sensual language by interpreting the song as an allegory. An allegory is a narrative that describes a subject but under the guise of another topic altogether. In an allegory, an object, thing or person comes to represent something else; for example, in the allegory in Judges 9 a thornbush represents Abimelech as the king. There the text offers clear clues to help the reader understand the elements in the allegory. The Song of Songs, on the other hand, gives no such indications or clues to help us understand it as an allegory. Therefore, an allegorical interpretation is inappropriate, for it leads to an arbitrary understanding of the elements in the song.

A very common allegorical approach to the song is to take it as a description of the relationship between God and his people. In the New Testament era, the young man has been understood to represent

Jesus Christ and the young woman represents the church of the Old and New Testaments. This interpretation, however, completely spiritualizes the song, and as a result it now does not say anything about the relationship between a man and woman in love, but it is solely about the relationship between God and his people.

Challenges in interpretation

This song presents a number of challenges for interpretation. An important consideration is that this song is a poem. Poetry uses artistic expression to convey moods, feelings and ideas. The language of poetry is never as precise as that of prose, which is the straightforward way in which we normally speak to each other and that communicates our message more directly. Poetry, on the other hand, attempts to communicate feelings and emotions. Since poetry deals with imagery, it can often convey different perceptions to different readers. It is also challenging to understand certain poetic expressions, either because they are so old that their meaning has been lost, or because they can be understood in different ways.

In this song the modern reader meets a couple living in a completely different cultural setting from ours today. The expressions of love this couple use often seem strange, for it is language that we never use when expressing our love and therefore it can be a challenge to grasp the emotions and feelings being conveyed. In addition, when a couple expresses their love for each other they often use terms and phrases that are personal to them and seem outlandish or strange to anyone else. These things cause the mood or feelings being conveyed to be a challenge for us to interpret.

We also need to keep in mind that poetic language allows the text to carry different levels of meaning—there can be a literal level as well as allusions to other possible interpretations. For example, in one incident the woman invites her husband to come into her garden. We could interpret this literally, that she is inviting him to enjoy the garden that she has planted, but she may be referring to her body and using the imagery of a garden to invite her husband to come and enjoy her body. Such allusions and hidden meanings are part of the nature of poetry.

Different interpretations of a particular text or passage of the song may be possible, but it is important that we always interpret the text within the context of the whole of scripture. Here I take a fundamentally different approach from those who approach the Song of Songs as a piece of literature independent from the rest of scripture. If the whole of scripture is understood to be God's Word of revelation, then we must see how this song throws light on other parts of scripture and how other parts of scripture give us a better understanding of this song. It should become clear in our interpretation how this book reflects the great message of redemption. Together with the rest of scripture, this song gives us a fuller understanding and appreciation of God's command to show love not only in marriage, but also in our relationship with Jesus Christ as our bridegroom.[3]

Chapter 1

The Man for You

Let him kiss me with the kisses of his mouth—
for your love is more delightful than wine.
Pleasing is the fragrance of your perfumes;
your name is like perfume poured out.
No wonder the young women love you!
Take me away with you—let us hurry!
Let the king bring me into his chambers.

We rejoice and delight in you;
we will praise your love more than wine.

How right they are to adore you!
(Song of Songs 1:2–4)

*I*t is only natural that in the course of life there is a time when the minds of men and women turn to thoughts of love and romance. Every person at some time dreams about falling in love. What do you imagine the person of your dreams will be like? Do you already have in mind the kind of person you are looking for? How will you decide on the kind of man or woman you want? Maybe the person you dream about looks somewhat like the one who graces the cover of a current fashion magazine. Maybe you dream about someone who is rich and famous. In the first lines of this song, the woman speaks to the man she loves and her words reveal many things about her. The things that she appreciates in him reflect her own values, and as we come to understand those values we realize that this is a woman with wisdom—someone whose words give us some direction as to the kind of man that a woman desiring genuine love and a lasting relationship should look for.

In the opening words of the song the woman conveys three basic thoughts. In the first place, her words reveal how natural it is for a man and woman to feel a passionate desire for each other; couples may celebrate their love for each other and long for the day of the consummation of that love. Secondly, the reason she loves this man is because she can fully trust him. She has not only discovered this for herself but others confirm that he has an excellent reputation. And finally, her love for him means that she wants to honour him by respecting the role that the Lord has given him; love blossoms when husbands and wives respect the roles the Lord gives to them in marriage.

Desire awakened

The opening lines of this song are quite startling. Strong emotions and passionate desires are expressed vividly right at the very beginning. We might consider the passionate language this woman uses to convey her deep love for this man to be rather shocking, the expressions coming at what seems to us to be just the beginning of their relationship (we haven't even met the guy yet!). The sensual language used might also make us uncomfortable, since our perspective on this aspect of our life has been distorted by sin. After Adam and Eve fell into sin they were ashamed of their nakedness and sewed together fig leaves as clothing. But when God restores the relationship with his people, he makes it possible for them to enjoy the sensual aspect of their marriage without any shame. The joyful expression of love and passionate desire at the very beginning sets the tone for the whole song. Therefore, the first words of this song are preparing us for what is to follow (Garrett 128). It introduces the song as a love song that is a joyous celebration of love. The song will develop themes of love, passion and marriage.

The woman's first words are, "Let him kiss me with the kisses of his mouth—for your love is more delightful than wine." She is thinking about the joy of having him kiss her with the passionate kisses of those in love with each other. She wants to experience what his kiss will arouse within her. She says, "Your love is more delightful than wine." Comparing the intoxicating effect of wine to the intoxicating effect of his kisses, she declares that the passion his kisses arouse in her is "more delightful" than the intoxicating effect of wine. She continues along the same line in verse 3, speaking of the euphoric sensations this man evokes in her: "Pleasing is the fragrance of your perfumes; your name is like perfume poured out." She longs to be close to him so that she can smell the fragrance of his cologne. But when he is not with her, she can still sense this fragrance, and it is a constant reminder of him so that it is as if he is always with her.

Those who have experienced love understand those things—the heady, overwhelming effect of that first attraction. But the woman next takes things in what, to us, is a shocking direction. She is so totally carried away by her longing for him that she demands in verse 4, "Take me away with you—let us hurry! Let the king bring me into his chambers." This is not just a strong wish, but she is giving a strong command. In her passion she is demanding that he take her away—literally, that he must drag her away with him. And she wants this to happen right now! What is she really asking? She wants him to take her away to some private place so that they can explore their love.

While the first line was a command for him to take her away quickly, the second line seems to indicate that she is already there, in his inner chamber. The second line literally says, "The king has brought me into his chambers." To resolve what sounds like an inconsistency here, the New International Version (NIV) translates the second line as a wish, "Let the king bring me into his chambers," making her words a command for him to take her away into his chambers.

She refers to the man as "the king," which might be confusing. While some think that this is a reference to King Solomon, there is an explanation that fits the context of this song better. Bergant notes that it was a common practice during wedding ceremonies in the ancient Near East to call the bride and groom "king and queen" for the day (*Song of Songs* 11). Therefore, it would be very natural for a woman to speak about the man she loves as her king. A king protects and provides for his people, and that is what she wants him to do for her. She wants her beloved, her king, to take her to his chamber, an inner room where they can find privacy.

As opening words to a love song, these are pretty strong sentiments. This woman is already thinking about being in her beloved's inner chamber, or bedroom even, where she can enjoy a time of intimacy with him. But these verses are actually introducing us to what is to follow and preparing us for where the Song of Songs is going. The song begins with a couple that is passionately in love and wanting some time away so that they might explore their love for each other in privacy. When love is awakened it quite naturally grows into a desire for an intimate marriage relationship. The passionate words of the song reflect the power that love has to awaken strong desires in a person. The powerful emotions and strong desires that this woman expresses are a mystery that no one can really understand or explain, but we know that they are real because we certainly experience it! This is something that God has created in us, and we simply accept it as a God-given gift, not something to be ashamed of or that needs to be hidden.

In the past, the church has taught that sexual desires are evil and shameful, a perspective which has yielded some unfortunate outcomes. First, it results in an unhealthy way of thinking about sexuality that at times has negatively impacted the sexual relationship between husbands and wives. Also, the awakening sexual desires of maturing young men and women have been regarded as sinful and therefore need to be quashed. But the Lord created us as sexual human beings, and those strong passions should be understood as a gift from the Lord and part of his plan for bringing young men and women to desire each other in marriage. The fact that the church has not always been straightforward and accurate or positive in its teaching about human sexuality means that God's people have often been confused about this aspect of their lives. But by not presenting human sexuality as God's gift, many opportunities have been left open for God's people to misuse and abuse this gift. Sexual desire separated from love and taken out of the context in which God intended it to function becomes a great evil. Sexual desire is such a powerful emotion—it is so easy to let those desires run out of control, and separated from true love the desires become an idol that takes control of one's soul, something that Satan manipulates for evil purposes.

Today's culture thrives on sex, but most people do not understand the negative impact that misuse of sex has on our relationships. Today, sex is basically used either as a marketing tool, to sell goods or as a form of entertainment. The retail industry knows that sex appeal sells products and it is not shy about using sex to the fullest advantage. When it comes to entertainment, Hollywood learned long ago that sex brings an audience to movies. And as another form of entertainment, pornography is a huge industry today. For a long time, pornography was considered to be part of the dirty underbelly of our society, but it has become mainstream. Although there are voices warning about the exploitation of men and women by this industry, generally society has accepted pornography as an innocent form of entertainment and refuses to see how it twists and warps the desires of human beings.

When we use sex as a form of entertainment it develops unrealistic expectations in us regarding sexuality. When our husband or wife does not compare favourably to the attractive models we are used to seeing, it leads to dissatisfaction in the marriage relationship. Whether we think about sex as it is used to sell products or as it is used for entertainment, the effects are the same. When people become the objects of physical pleasure for others, then the result is that they are no longer thought of as human beings but as objects of pleasure. The sex industry is about fulfilling the lust of the heart, and that type of lust can never be satisfied so there is always a greater demand for sexually explicit material.[1] When sex becomes such a force in your life, affecting your choices and actions and expectations, it has become the idol to which you submit your life.

Surrounded as we are by today's highly sexualized culture, it is difficult to keep the wonderful gift of human sexuality pure and as God intended it. Sexuality is such a powerful passion that it is also easy to become trapped in its vices. When Balaam was unable to place a curse on Israel to destroy that nation, he advised the people of Moab that the sure way to destroy Israel was to entice them with Moabite women. And sure enough, the men of Israel "began to indulge in sexual immorality with Moabite women who invited them..." (Numbers 25:1, 2; 31:16). We must always guard against the misuse of the wonderful gift of sexuality.

The passionate words of the Song of Songs remind us first of all about the great beauty of sexuality. When used properly by a man and a woman seeking to love each other passionately as God intended them to, it is a most wonderful and precious gift. But because of sin, love can so easily turn to lust that damages our marriage relationship. When a husband's only concern is to satisfy his own sexual needs and he does not lovingly care for the needs of his wife, he has allowed lust to take control in the relationship. In his Word, the Lord God reveals to us his tender love that is the basis for the love a husband and wife can again experience. God reveals his love in the way he compassionately cares for his people. He often compares his own relationship with Israel to a marriage relationship where in his great mercy and love he tenderly cares for his people and encourages them to live with him in a faithful and loving relationship. Therefore, this song reflects the truth that genuine love between a man and woman in marriage must be based on the love of God for his people. From a New Testament perspective, Christ came and revealed himself as the great bridegroom who has chosen his church to be his bride. Christ's relationship with us is the basis on which we must learn to love one another. The more we understand the love of Christ for his bride, the more it will impact our marriages. A husband and wife can only experience true love if they first experience the love of Christ.

A good reputation: precious

The opening words of the song establish that this woman is passionately in love and that she wants the relationship with this man to develop into marriage. But these passionate words also tell something about the character of this man and woman. She seems to know her beloved very well, for she says in verse 3, "Pleasing is the fragrance of your perfumes; your name is like perfume poured out." We can paraphrase her words to say, "Like the fragrance of his perfume that radiates from his body, so the fragrant aroma of his name emanates from him." In scripture, the word "name" often refers to a person's reputation. Her words tell us that this man has a good reputation so that everyone speaks highly of him and looks to him with respect. She likes his perfume, but she really likes his character even more. Her love for him is not simply based on sexual attraction; she loves the kind of man he is.

She does not go into great detail about his character, but it is clear that she regards him as a man of upstanding moral quality because he is a man of good reputation. Perhaps at this point in their relationship she might know this from her own experience with him, but if it is a new relationship she might feel confident about him because of what others think of him. She says in 1:3, "No wonder that the maidens love you!" These maidens, or young women, are probably the same ones who later, in 1:4, say, "We rejoice and delight in you; we will praise your love more than wine." She has talked to these women and they agree with her that this man is respectable and trustworthy. And so she says, "How right those maidens are to adore you, for they know what kind of person you are."

These opening verses reveal the kind of man this woman admires, giving us an example of what a godly woman should admire and look for in a man. She does not explicitly lay out all his moral attributes, as more details will emerge later in the song, but it is clear that he has particular qualities that attract her to him. This woman finds great confidence in knowing that the man she loves has a good reputation. Every godly woman should discover that the man she has set her heart on has a good reputation.

For men, these verses reveal how important it is to develop a godly character so that others, also the women who know you, can speak about your good reputation. There is nothing better than to be a pleasing fragrance that is attractive to the woman you love. You should be attractive because you display godly values that are the result of your heartfelt commitment to Christ. Your commitment to Christ will change the priority in your life to serving the Lord. It should be more important, for the sake of Christ, to develop a good reputation than it is to follow the desires of your own heart. Sometimes we need to ask ourselves the following sorts of questions:

What kind of reputation do I have? When people talk about me, what will they talk about? Will they remember the times I got drunk and did outrageous things? Will they talk about my arrogance and boasting, or will they remember my sexual and irreverent talk? Will they think about me as a womanizer who likes flirting with the girls? You should wonder if people speak of you in a respectful way—about what kind of fragrance your name gives off.

I think you will agree that a bad reputation is not the kind of reputation you want to have as a Christian. What Christian woman or man in her or his right mind wants to live in a fragrance that gives off the stench of decay? Is that what you want to be for the one you love? I don't think so! When you think of Christ's reputation, consider how it spreads out from him as a pleasing fragrance that is enjoyed by everyone who serves him in love. Does the way Christ lived for you not say something about how you should live for him? Christ showed in his own life the great value of having a good reputation. No wonder Ecclesiastes 7:1 says, "A good name is better than fine perfume."

The woman of this song reminds us how important it is for men to cultivate a good reputation. You cultivate such a reputation by living as a faithful child of God who rejoices at being redeemed by the blood of Christ. When women get to know you, they should also be able to discern that you are faithful, responsible and dependable. They should know by your reputation that you truly care for others and that, therefore, you are someone who is to be desired.

Roles respected

Remember how in the opening words of the song the woman commands the man she loves to take her away with him. Her bold action raises a question about her role in the relationship. Here the woman speaks first and she takes the initiative, demanding, "Let him kiss me," and "Take me away with you—hurry!" While her words might not sound so shocking by today's standards, she does seem to break out of the cultural mould of her time, one in which men were usually dominant in relationships (Provan 272). In the culture of the ancient Near East the man owned his wife, and a woman did whatever her husband demanded. Women tended to be passive in the relationship. This woman, however, is anything but passive, for she takes the initiative. Some argue that she is breaking free from the dominance of the man (Provan 275). She sees herself as equal to him, and therefore she has the right to make demands on him. Some commentators take this a step further and see a reversal in the roles between husband and wife, regarding her as a modern-type feminist.[2] I believe that this interpretation does not do justice to what is being taught in this song, but it does direct our attention to something important here.

The seemingly bold action of this woman actually reveals that the relationship between them is being restored by God to the way it was in the Garden of Eden before the fall into sin. God promised Adam and Eve after the fall into sin that he would give them a son who would bring about a great restoration in this world (Genesis 3:15). On the basis of this promise, and long before Christ appeared, God was already restoring the relationship not only between himself and his people but also between believers and their fellow human beings. In this incident in the song we see the Lord already making it possible for this woman to experience liberation from the tyranny of a man who is normally under the effect of sin. When true love as God intended it is restored in the relationship between a man and woman, the effects of sin and corruption begin to fall away. Then the man and woman will be equal in the relationship so that neither has the desire to dominate the other. In this love relationship, a woman will feel the wonderful liberty of being able to freely approach the man she loves and to demand his love in return. She feels no shame in taking the initiative, asking him for his passionate kisses and demanding that he take her into his chamber where she can experience his love. With genuine love, the wall that sin and corruption set up in a relationship is torn down and a man and woman are able to treat each other with love and respect.

Although the woman takes the initiative in these opening verses, it is instructive to see how she does so. She takes an active role in speaking, yet she honours him as her head with her words.[3] She commands him to take the lead in the way she expresses her desire for his kisses. She does not say, "I will kiss him," but she says, "Let him kiss me." The same is seen when she commands him to "Take me away with you." She does not say, "I will take you into my chamber," but she expects him to lead and commands him to take her into his chamber. She experiences freedom in her relationship with this man and yet she also maintains the roles that God has given for the relationship. A Christian woman is not looking for a man that she can dominate. She will not find any joy in such a man because he cannot give her the security, guidance and care that she desires. She is looking for a man that she can look up to with respect, a man who gives spiritual guidance, one who is willing to take the initiative and lead, one whose love is loyal and faithful and tender and one who is willing to give up everything for her well-being. That is the mystery of love. A woman looks for a man who can be respected but not dominated. Therefore, young men, you need to equip yourself spiritually so that you are ready to provide spiritual leadership in a loving relationship. What the woman in the song is looking for is not someone who forces his will on her, uses her for his pleasure and treats her as his property. She desires a man who will lead her in the ways of the Lord, a man who seriously wants to protect her and care for her the rest of her life. That is the man of her dreams, and that should be the man of every woman's dreams. She wants a man she can command to take her into his bedchamber, because there she knows she will be safe and secure in his arms.

This woman desires a relationship that is a clear reflection of our relationship with Jesus Christ. As the bride of Christ,[4] we are free to make demands on him as our bridegroom; you may demand from Jesus his love, and in a time of need you may ask him to protect and strengthen you. Because of his great love for you, revealed through his sacrifice on the cross, you can, without any reservation or hesitation, call upon him for his help. You can do this confidently, trusting that he will respond because of his love for you. As the bride of Christ, you may demand that he take you away with him into his eternal kingdom of glory. He will take the lead as a faithful bridegroom. It is this relationship with Christ that must become the pattern that develops in your love relationship. A woman in a relationship should feel great confidence that she will never be rejected or hurt by her beloved. When there is genuine love you will also have the freedom to be open with one another—to expose all your needs and the deepest concerns of your heart. You can do so because you trust that the one who loves you will protect you and care for you. True love, patterned after the love of Christ, is truly liberating, for it gives you a wonderful environment for your love to grow and blossom as you learn to serve the Lord together.

For Further Reflection

1. Discuss why the song begins with strong, sensual language and how it prepares us for the themes that will follow. Does this say something about God's intention for marriage?

2. The woman commands her beloved to take her to his inner chamber because she desires a moment of intimacy. Discuss how this sensual language teaches us to think about love and the desires it awakens in a man and woman.

3. What kind of negative impacts can the stance that sexual desires are evil and sinful have on the life of God's people? How should young men and woman deal with the awakening of sexual desires?

4. What are the challenges that God's people face in an increasingly sexualized world? Discuss means of protecting oneself from the negative impact of those challenges.

5. Discuss how God reveals his tender love for his people, Israel, and how God's love becomes the basis for the love between a husband and wife.

6. Why is it important that the man this woman loves has a good reputation, which is like perfume poured out? How does this indicate that love is about more than sexual attraction?

7. Discuss what kind of reputation godly men should strive to develop, that will be attractive to godly women.

8. What kind of reputation does Christ have, and how does that attract you to him as your Lord?

9. What does the fact that the woman takes the initiative in the opening words teach us about the roles between husbands and wives? How does the woman still honour her husband as her head and maintain his role in the relationship? Discuss what this reveals about how God intended the marriage relationship to function before the fall in sin.

10. Why does the woman not desire a man that she can dominate? What does this say about the need for men to develop proper leadership skills, and what are some of those skills? What does this say about our relationship with Christ and how he leads his bride, the church?

Chapter 2

The Woman for You

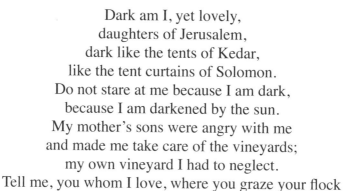

Dark am I, yet lovely,
daughters of Jerusalem,
dark like the tents of Kedar,
like the tent curtains of Solomon.
Do not stare at me because I am dark,
because I am darkened by the sun.
My mother's sons were angry with me
and made me take care of the vineyards;
my own vineyard I had to neglect.
Tell me, you whom I love, where you graze your flock
and where you rest your sheep at midday.
Why should I be like a veiled woman beside the flocks of
your friends?

If you do not know, most beautiful of women,
follow the tracks of the sheep and graze your young goats
by the tents of the shepherds.
(Song of Songs 1:5–8)

*I*n this part of the song the woman clearly feels defensive on account of the glances of the daughters of Jerusalem. This is such a contrast to the confident tone of the first four verses of the song, spoken by the same woman. A group from another "culture," girls from the city, is making the speaker feel her inadequacy as a woman. We've all experienced similar feelings of inadequacy brought on by the reaction of others, or we have made others feel this way by our attitude towards them. Because these city girls are making her feel uncomfortable, this woman says to them, "Do not stare at me because I am dark, because I am darkened by the sun" (verse 6). Her self-description reveals something about her character, things that every Christian woman should seek to develop in her own life, qualities which young men would do well to find when considering a life partner.

Young men and women need to reflect on the kind of relationship they should seek. Too often people pursue relationships without thinking about what the nature of that relationship should be, instead following the momentary fancies of their heart. It is not unusual for a young man to go through a time in which the girl of his dreams is someone like a beautiful model or famous beauty from the entertainment industry. Reality usually begins to set in quickly as he realizes that such dreams are unrealistic. Men (as well as women) need to think about the things that are important in a relationship before they begin dating.

Serious thought needs to be put into a dating decision. You need to ask yourself about your motives and goals in dating this girl or boy. Dating is not merely a sport in which you just go out to have a good time, nor is it an outing for which you chose an object to be seen with—someone that you think might enhance your stature. I do not mean that dating cannot be fun—dating should be an enjoyable experience—but you must also understand that dating is a significant step. Dating is an opportunity to get to know someone and to test whether that person displays the godly qualities necessary for marriage. You want to learn whether you can function together in a lifelong relationship in which you both desire to give glory to God. For a marriage to work, a couple needs to begin the relationship on common ground—the desire to root their life in the life of Jesus Christ. On that basis the relationship can grow with confidence, because the couple realizes that they cannot go forward in their own strength but only in the strength of the Lord.

Therefore, it is important that young men and women understand the qualities that are essential for a spouse. One cannot expect to find a perfect person—the result of sin is that we are all flawed human beings who struggle with the selfish desires of our own hearts. Yet, in the life of the woman in this song, the Lord reveals some basic characteristics that are important for the life of every woman and gives insight into what a young man should see in a possible life partner. In her self-description in these verses, the woman reveals three characteristics that make her attractive to her beloved and which we will look at in this chapter. She displays a depth of substance and godly humility, as well as a sense of discretion.

A woman of substance

In describing her appearance in 1:5-8, the young woman reveals a little about her life situation and offers a glimpse of the kind of girl she is. Some of her characteristics begin to stand out through the contrast with the more superficial qualities of the "daughters of Jerusalem." There is much speculation about the identity of these daughters of Jerusalem who appear more often in this song (2:7; 3:5, 10, 11; 5:8, 16; 8:4), but there is no evidence in the song to support any definitive conclusion. In the song, the daughters of Jerusalem appear to function as a poetic device useful in making a point. The contrast between the girls who come from the city and the woman of the song who comes from the country is a familiar theme in literature. City girls are thought to be, or tend to think they are, more sophisticated than country girls (Keel 49). Here, the city girls are used as a foil against which the values of the main character of the song are highlighted.

First, the woman says that her skin is like the colour of the tents of Kedar, a powerful nomadic tribe.[1] It is likely that their tents were made from tanned hides or woven cloth that were dark in colour, or weathered. She does not only describe herself with the less-than-positive image of the dark material of the tents of Kedar, but she continues by contrasting her complexion to the tent curtains of Solomon. As a king, Solomon's tents were likely a deep purple, the colour of royalty, and so she compares her colouring to the rich darkness of those curtains. This reference to Solomon invokes the splendour and beauty of that wealthy king's palaces, suggesting by extension that her dark complexion could also be lovely. Therefore, what she may very well be saying is that she is as sturdy as the tents of Kedar and that she has a lovely, rich colouring like the glorious splendour of Solomon's tent.

Her complexion obviously was not considered fashionable for it attracted the glances of the daughters of Jerusalem, and so she says to them, "Do not stare at me because I am dark, because I am darkened by the sun." Many have suggested that she is saying she is from a black ethnic background, but her own words are that the sun has darkened her skin because her brothers have made her work hard in the family vineyard. When she works in the open vineyard the sun beats down on her so that her skin is tanned and perhaps she has even burned at times in the blistering heat of the day.

She is conscious of the fact that her dark complexion makes her stand out among the girls of the city, and she also understands that this colouring and the work that caused it set her apart from these city girls who have a completely different kind of life. Sheltered from the hard life of the country, they are mainly concerned about their own appearance. The women's words indicate that they, unlike her, are able to take precautions against the sun and we can easily imagine them being preoccupied with making up their faces and doing up their hair instead of spending their time with the necessary chores of life. In contrast, this woman from the country says in 1:6 that her brothers make her work in the family vineyard so that "my own vineyard I have neglected."

One interpretation is that she owns her own vineyard but has neglected it because her brothers have forced her to work in the family vineyard. Such a meaning is unlikely since it was rare for a woman in Israel to own a vineyard, and it would be strange that she would own her own vineyard while her family owns another in which she has to work. More likely she is using the image of the vineyard to speak about herself. The metaphor of a vineyard is used more often in scripture to describe a person or even the nation of Israel. Later in this song, the woman will compare her body to a garden (4:12). In this poetic way she tells us that she has been so busy working in the family's vineyard that she has not had time to pamper herself or be concerned about how others might judge her appearance. The fact that she has not been able to conform to society's standards of beauty because of her commitment to care for the family vineyard does not bother her, because she says, in effect, "I will be myself and I will not be ashamed of that." She states confidently, "Dark am I, yet lovely," not allowing her suntanned complexion to let her believe that she is somehow less than the city girls with their superior attitude. She may have a suntan while they are lily-white but she recognizes her own beauty. She believes that true beauty is not determined by outward appearance, but is judged on the basis of things much deeper. And therefore, although she may be somewhat self-conscious when the city girls stare at her, she is not ashamed of her own appearance.

It would be incorrect to suggest that she does not care about how she looks or that it is not important to her to take care of her appearance and feel good about herself. She speaks about herself as "being lovely." Pride in appearance and the self-respect this reveals are important for a Christian woman. Most of us find it difficult to respect someone who has neglected his or her appearance. But at the same time that she takes pride in her appearance, this woman does not allow others, in this case the daughters of Jerusalem and their values, to set the standards for her. For her, having a pale complexion is less important than being busy in her family's vineyard. She will not let conformity to cultural standards stand in the way of what is required of her.

Wisdom, in Proverbs 31:30, says, "Charm is deceptive, and beauty is fleeting; but a woman who fears the Lord is to be praised." What society considers beautiful, wisdom describes as fleeting and deceptive. Today, those considered to be the most beautiful women in the world, those whose faces grace the covers of magazines, discover that their beauty is but fleeting and in a few short years, as their beauty fades away, they will be replaced by younger women. Popular standards of physical beauty are not a basis on which to build self-confidence or a lasting relationship. The woman in the song is not intimidated by the pressure from the daughters of Jerusalem and by accepting God's standards, she exhibits an inner beauty that flows out of faith in the Lord God. Her beauty will not only shine in the time of youth but also ten, twenty, fifty or even sixty years later. Inner beauty built on faith only becomes more glorious over time. The woman of this song is an encouragement for young women to value and develop that inner beauty of faith.

A girl who is primarily concerned with herself and places her confidence in her good looks will be challenged in contributing to a lasting relationship. The kind of woman who will be a great blessing is instead someone who loves to serve the Lord and puts him first in her life. She is willing to ignore the shallow values of society, and she will take pride in doing what is right even when others ridicule her for that. Such a woman will be a suitable helper for any man (Genesis 2:18), supporting him and encouraging him to be faithful in his God-given calling.

A woman of humility

The same words used by the woman in 1:6 that reveal something about the depth of her character also reveal something else about her character. She says, "My mother's sons were angry with me and made me take care of the vineyards; my own vineyard I have neglected." It is clear that the situation at her home was not ideal. She speaks about brothers but says nothing about a father. Her father is never mentioned in this song, while her brothers appear to have authority over the household. It is noteworthy that she does not speak about her brothers as "brothers," but refers to them as her "mother's sons," perhaps using this awkward expression to distance herself from them and to show that she is not very happy with them. She does not tell us why they are angry with her, but clearly the situation at home is not harmonious and her words indicate that she feels unjustly treated.

While one might argue that she had no choice in this matter since she was expected to carry out her brothers' wishes, yet her reaction tells us something more about her. It reveals a woman of faith who submits her life to God's will even when she feels that she is being treated unjustly. She is respectful of her role in the family and understands her responsibility. Although her brothers make her life difficult, yet she is devoted to her family. One commentator observes that "this builds on the important theme of commitment that is part of the love expressed throughout the song" (Hess 58, footnote 35). In spite of the treatment by her brothers, her commitment to the family means that she carries out her responsibilities in the vineyard. Fulfilling this responsibility in her family serves to build her character and reputation. Instead of insisting on her rights, she displays a sense of humility. She is willing to endure some injustice for the sake of her family and her Lord.

This humility is an important quality, for it is the attitude of humility that makes it possible for one to enter into a lifetime commitment with another. The young man in the song can truly love and respect this woman, confident that she can contribute to a strong relationship in which they will be committed to each other for the rest of their lives. She is not someone who demands or insists on getting her way in everything, nor does she make all kinds of demands on others. This is the attitude that young adults need to cultivate in their own lives. If by nature you are a demanding person and always insist on your own way, you will find marriage (for that matter, any relationship) to be extremely difficult. True love requires a humble commitment to your relationship even when it may seem to be a challenge to do so.

In the woman's complaint against her brothers, we can again hear her longing for the man she loves. Her words reveal a contrast between the way her brothers treat her and how she expects that the man she loves will treat her. Her brothers are acting unjustly towards her, but there is a man who loves and cherishes her. This is a man who fears God and does not abuse his power or authority over her. This is the man to whom she wants to commit herself for the rest of her life because she knows that she will be secure in his love.

A woman of discretion

The young woman says in 1:7, "Tell me, you whom I love, where you graze your flock and where you rest your sheep at midday. Why should I be like a veiled woman beside the flocks of your friends?" She says to the man she loves that she wants to meet him during the siesta at midday. It is quite natural for a couple newly fallen in love to look for opportunities to meet together. She asks the one she loves to give her directions to the place where he rests his sheep at noon because she does not want to furtively go from shepherd to shepherd looking for him, or to "be like a veiled woman" asking about his whereabouts.

While there is much discussion among commentators about the significance of her being like a veiled woman, what is clear is that she says to the man she loves that she does not want others to think about her as if she is like such a veiled woman. She wants to find him but she wants to do so with a sense of propriety. If he does not give her specific directions, then she will be wandering blindly in search of him and she will be in danger of being mistaken for a prostitute who is plying her trade among the other shepherds (Gledhill 108). While it is true that not all veiled women were prostitutes and that not all prostitutes were veiled as Tamar is described in Genesis 38:15, yet the implication here is that she does not want to feel the shame of being considered a prostitute by others. She refuses, through her actions, to risk her integrity and reputation in order to find her beloved. She risks her reputation not by being with the man she loves, but by blindly wandering from shepherd to shepherd so that people wonder about her intentions.

This woman has deeply held convictions and refuses to compromise her reputation to fulfill an impulse of the heart. The woman of this song reminds us of the fact that service to the Lord and commitment to his will are more important than compromising those principles, even if this means she cannot be with the man on whom she has set her heart. This reminds us that women (as well as men) must act wisely when dating in order not to regret any decisions later. If it is more important to have a relationship than to follow the principles that the Lord has given for our relationship, there is a very good chance that one will make unwise choices. The sad reality is that many who have acted on impulse rather than on principle have regretted the decisions they have made about a relationship. There are too many sad stories of relationships gone wrong when decisions are made on the basis of one's own desires and perhaps a feeling of desperation, for these often lead to misery. When you live by faith you will seek out a suitable marriage partner and trust that the Lord will provide.

Now, you might wonder, how can anyone hold on to the principles given by God if their heart is set on someone who is not a suitable marriage partner as defined by the principles given by God? How can one resist such a strong pull on the heart? The only way to hold on to those godly principles, as this young woman did, is to hold on to Jesus Christ. Our great encouragement is that, ultimately, Jesus Christ is our bridegroom. He gave his life for us on the cross and therefore we may completely trust him to take care of our lives. It is only possible to maintain discretion when you trust that your own life is in the loving care of the Lord Jesus. When you are in a living relationship with Christ, then he will always come first in your life. You will put him first because you trust with your whole heart that your life is secure with Christ and that you can count on his presence even in times of great loneliness.

Keep in mind that it will only be possible to find a spouse who holds dear the same principles you do if you remain faithful to Jesus Christ yourself. Remember that faithful Christian men are attracted to women who hold on to their Christian values. For both men and women, if you destroy your reputation, you also push away the kind of spouse that you desire.

It is dangerous to allow desperation to determine dating decisions. In 1:8 the woman receives some advice that is still important for young women today. In 1:7–8 she wonders how she will find the one she loves. She is advised (there is some question as to who is giving her advice; some think it is the young man himself, some think it is the girls from the city, or it may simply be an editorial comment)[2] to follow the sheep and graze her young goats by the tents of the shepherds; in other words, just go about her regular daily business. She should just take the young goats and let them graze by the tents of the shepherds, as she would normally do. As she cares for the young goats she will come into contact with the shepherd who is dear to her heart, and it will happen in a way that will not give others any reason to gossip about her actions. They will praise her for her dedication to her work. The poet appears to be making the point that she will not find the one she loves by flaunting herself like a loose woman among the shepherds, but instead by faithfully doing her daily work among them.

What this woman desires is also what Jesus Christ desires in the life of his bride, which is his church. The Lord Jesus wants you as his bride to live by faith and to refuse to compromise your Christian principles. As the great bridegroom, Christ calls you, his bride, to be a person of substance who is ready to give your whole heart to him. You are called to submit in humility to your bridegroom Jesus Christ, for in his great love he has bought you with his blood. And therefore young men and women also need to be faithful to Jesus Christ in the way they date. If you love to serve Christ then you will also look for a partner with whom you are one in Christ so that together you can sing the Song of Songs with your whole heart. In such a relationship you will enjoy the blessing of the Lord.

For Further Reflection

1. Discuss the kind of man or woman that you seek as a marriage partner. How will you determine the characteristics you are looking for? What are some of the characteristics that are important to you?

2. Discuss the purpose for dating and what you are looking for when you date.

3. How does the woman in the song reveal that she is a woman with substance when compared to the daughters of Jerusalem? What are the true standards of beauty?

4. Discuss the spirit of humility this woman displays in her reaction to the treatment of her brothers. Why is this spirit of humility necessary for a marriage commitment?

5. How does her brothers' treatment contrast to the expectation she has of how she will be treated by her beloved?

6. How does the woman in the song reveal a spirit of discretion? Does this spirit of discretion guide you in how you behave towards one another when you are dating? Discuss the importance of protecting each other's reputation in the relationship and how you will do that.

Chapter 3

Love That Flourishes

I liken you, my darling,
to a mare among Pharaoh's chariot horses.
Your cheeks are beautiful with earrings,
your neck with strings of jewels.
We will make you earrings of gold,
studded with silver.

While the king was at his table,
my perfume spread its fragrance.
My beloved is to me a sachet of myrrh
resting between my breasts.
My beloved is to me a cluster of henna blossoms
from the vineyards of En Gedi.
(Song of Songs 1:9–14)

*U*ntil this point, there has been one voice in the song—that of the woman.[1] This section, however, begins with a few lines of poetry by the man who is the recipient of the woman's admiration, her beloved. In the lines of verse 9, the man responds to her passionate words by declaring his love for her. Now, with the introduction of both parties, a dialogue begins that reveals a developing relationship. Here they speak to each other about the love that already exists between them, and through this communication they nourish their love for each other.

The couple expresses their love for each other in poetic language. Their expressions will sound strange to our ears as we are not accustomed to describing our love in ways that were probably common to their time. The reality is that couples then, just as they do now, often developed their own love language to convey their feelings for one another. Perhaps you can think of some expressions you and your beloved use to convey love for each other in your relationship. If others were to listen they may wonder at your choice of language, but you understand each other very well. In the same way, this couple has their own way of expressing their love for each other.

A man's love

The man's first words of endearment are, "I liken you, my darling, to a mare among Pharaoh's chariot horses." As an expression of love and admiration, these words sound very strange indeed. Read within the context of that place and time, however, these words become special. In the ancient Near East, the horse was very highly prized as a symbol of power, as well as of grace and beauty. God had forbidden the kings of Israel to keep horses, not wanting his people to put their trust in the strength of horses instead of in the power of the Lord their God.[2] But the beauty of the animal and the status and power it symbolized proved irresistible to King Solomon who, in defiance of God's will, brought many horses into Israel through his contacts with Egypt.[3] Now, the man in the song describes the grace and beauty he sees in this woman with the image of a mare, imagery that is difficult for us today to fully appreciate, but from the context, the message he wants to convey becomes clear.

It has been suggested that it was Pharaoh's habit to ride out to meet his people in his kingdom, and when he did this he would ride in a chariot pulled by the most beautiful mare in his stable. This man is then comparing the woman he loves to the most beautiful mare in Pharaoh's stable, praising her for her beauty and grace. This is the interpretation followed by the NIV translation, but there is also good reason to think that normally it was a stallion, an unneutered male horse, that pulled Pharaoh's chariot. One commentator has noted that in all ancient Egyptian texts and pictures it is stallions and not mares that pull Pharaoh's chariots, referring to one example depicting Pharaoh's wife and daughter riding in a chariot that is pulled by a stallion (Keel 56–57). By all accounts, when the Egyptians went into battle, they only used stallions to pull their chariots, probably because of the strength and energy of these animals. Young stallions are virile animals also, so a mare placed among them would be a powerful distraction. There is one account of an Egyptian enemy sending a mare in heat out into the middle of the chariots, with predictable results (Pope 338–339).

Taken altogether, then, when the man says to this woman, "I liken you, my darling, to a mare among Pharaoh's chariot horses," he seems to be telling her that he is so enamored by her that he cannot focus on anything else but her, just like stallions are completely distracted by a mare placed in their midst. He is completely distracted by her presence and considers her to be the most beautiful woman in the whole world. He also declares, "Your cheeks are beautiful with earrings, your neck with strings of jewels," observing that her beauty is accentuated by the earrings that dangle over her cheeks and the necklace of jewels around her neck. Her beauty overwhelms him. The poetry suggests that he sees her inner qualities that enhance her physical beauty. He is not measuring her beauty against society's standards, but against God's. Genuine love sees a person for who they are inside, and it is those inner qualities that are endearing. Even though this woman's dark complexion (1:5) may not meet the standard of beauty set by the daughters of Jerusalem, in his eyes she is like a mare among the stallions, very distracting and the only one for whom he has eyes.

There are a number of lessons that men can learn from this man as he expresses his love for this woman. First of all, this is a lesson in the power and importance of expressing your love for the special woman in your life by telling her about the beauty you see in her. You would not speak like this to just any woman, but only to one who is very special to you. Whether in courtship or marriage, a man and woman in love only have eyes for each other, remaining totally loyal and faithful to each other. That loyalty and faithfulness is expressed in the words of endearment that are only spoken in such an intimate relationship. As a couple, you get to know each other, and as your relationship and love deepen it is important that a language of love that is unique to your relationship develops between you. You need to learn to express your love with words of endearment as the couple do in this song.

There is another important element of their relationship that comes to light in the words of this man. By expressing his love in this way, we see that the relationship has deepened as he tells this woman that she is very special and dear to him. No other girl compares to her, and as far as he is concerned, she is the most beautiful among all women. With these words, he is building up his beloved and giving her confidence. Her own words have already told us that she is aware that she does not measure up to the typical standards for beauty because of her dark complexion. But that insecurity is taken away by his description of her beauty. It gives her confidence to know that she is very special in his eyes. I have seen young girls struggling with insecurities who begin to blossom into confident young women when they begin a relationship with a man who loves them. This is another aspect of the wonderful way in which the Lord has created men and women. God has given each man a special role in nurturing that wonderful relationship with the special woman that God has brought into his life. You need to understand that you will either be a positive or a negative influence in the life of the woman you love. If you are negative and critical, or if you rarely compliment the one you love, you undermine her confidence and she will begin to question your love and herself. If the one you love is very special to you, you need to let her know that she is beautiful and that you love her very much.

This is not only true during your courtship but also in your marriage. Men can become busy and distracted with so many other things in their lives. There is the daily grind at work, commitments in the community or the church and meetings to attend. Often it's a sporting event you want to see or a round of golf you want to play or a fishing trip that is so important. Men can become so involved with all these things that they forget about nurturing the one who should be special in their life. We often act as if the women we love should know that we love them, and we wonder why they sometimes question our love, maybe even thinking, "How can you question my love when I do so much for you?" The things we do for each other are important, but love is also something that needs to be expressed from the heart.

Drawing an analogous connection to our relationship with the Lord God might be helpful here. Scripture reveals that prayer is a very important part of our response of love to God.[4] It is through your prayer that you express to the Lord both your love and devotion to him and your complete dependence on him. What the Lord wants first of all from us is our expression of love; and following that, our love will be shown in the way we serve him. That principle is also true for all our relationships and especially for our marriage relationship, where words of love for your spouse give him or her confidence and a sense of security. When you are positive towards the one you love and you encourage her with meaningful words of endearment, it helps her confidence to grow, for she knows that she is special in your eyes. If she knows that you truly care for her even when things are difficult, and that you truly love her even when you have disagreements, she will experience the joy of feeling secure in your love.

Having built up the woman's confidence and sense of security with his words of love, this man goes further still. He says to her in 1:11, "We will make you earrings of gold, studded with silver." He does not identify the "we" but perhaps he is referring to the craftsman who will make the jewellery to adorn the one he loves. There are some courting practices that have not changed over the ages; every man will remember going to the jewellery store at some time to buy something special for the girl he loves. He wants to give tangible proof of his love, and it gives him great pleasure to see his beloved adorn herself with the jewellery he has given her. This is a very natural way to express your love to the one you really care about.

What the man promises this woman is not so strange when you recall what Christ does for his church. Jesus Christ himself speaks words of endearment to his people and he promises to adorn his bride with wonderful gifts. The Lord God spoke to the Old Testament church already in this way in Ezekiel 16. He reminds his wayward people about his love for them when he describes, in 16:9–13, how when he found them abandoned like a newborn in the field:

> I bathed you with water and washed the blood from you and put ointments on you. I clothed you with an embroidered dress and put leather sandals on you. I dressed you in fine linen and covered you with costly garments. I adorned you with jewellery: I put brace- lets on your arms and a necklace around your neck, and I put a ring on your nose, earrings on your ears and a beautiful crown on your head. So you were adorned with gold and silver; your clothes were of fine linen and costly fabric and embroidered cloth. Your food was fine flour, honey and olive oil. You became very beautiful and rose to be a queen.

God is explaining here how there was no reason for Israel to question his love, because they just have to look at how he has show- ered them with many gifts and adorned them with precious jewel- lery. Today, Jesus Christ as the great bridegroom continues to adorn his church with wonderful gifts; he clothes her with his righteous- ness and adorns her with his Spirit. Paul says in Ephesians 5:27 that Christ's purpose is to present his bride to himself as a radiant church, without stain or wrinkle, but holy and blameless. Christ's love for his bride is so great that he will shower her with every spiritual blessing. His great love gives us the confidence to serve him with our whole heart and makes us radiant, for his display of love ensures us of our security in the embrace of his arms.

And as Paul says in Ephesians 5:28, just as Christ revealed his great love for his bride the church, "In the same way, husbands ought to love their wives." Christ makes it possible for men and women to again enjoy the love that he intended for us in the beginning in paradise. And so men must ask themselves, can the woman I love be confident in my love and can she experience a sense of security, well- being and peace in my arms? Or does she feel apprehensive because she is waiting for the next angry outburst or volatile moment? Men, if you want to see the one you love flourish, with your words and actions you need to create an environment in which she feels secure in your love. Her greatest joy is to feel completely safe and loved in your embrace.

A woman's love

Just as the man's words of love need to be understood in the context of the time they were written in before they make any sense to us, the woman's response in 1:12—"While the king was at his table, my perfume spread its fragrance. My beloved is to me a sachet of myrrh resting between my breasts"—also sounds a little unusual as an expression of love! First of all, she refers to the man she loves as the king. Some think she is referring to King Solomon here, but it is also an expression that was often used by women in Israel for the man whom they loved. It is a term of endearment that at the same time reveals the respect she has for her beloved. True love can only blossom when a woman is able to respect her beloved, as one would give respect to a king. To understand how a wife might look up to her husband as a king, it is helpful to see its parallel in our relationship with Christ. As the bride of Christ, we look up to him with loving respect and expect him to protect us as our faithful king. And for a woman to build a relationship with her beloved, she needs to be able to respect him, confident that he will always lovingly protect and care for her.

She expresses the confidence she has in his love for her when she says: "While the king was at his table my perfume spread its fragrance." Generally, as she points out, any man remembers with great delight the fragrance worn by his girlfriend, and the smell of that fragrance immediately reminds him of her. But in 1:13 she turns that around as she describes her beloved as her perfume. In those days, they did not have the modern convenience of sticks of deodorant that can just be wiped on. Instead, a woman would have worn a little bag, a sachet, of herbs around her neck, to act as a fragrant perfume. Therefore, referring to that sachet, she says, "My lover is to me a sachet of myrrh resting between my breasts." She desires that this wonderful man would always be with her, just like that sachet of perfume. In the same way that she always has the scent of her perfume about her, the pleasant aroma of her beloved is always with her. This is an image of how this man is constantly on her mind, just as he had expressed earlier that his mind was constantly distracted by his thoughts of her.

It is very natural for any couple to come to a point in their relationship, once they begin to know each other better, when they seem to only have thoughts about each other. Family members can even grow tired of listening to a son or daughter or sibling who has fallen in love, because that person constantly speaks about their boyfriend or girlfriend. In no other human relationship do you find that kind of intensity. The Lord created a man and woman so that they naturally have this desire for one another. Moses, in an editorial note in Genesis 2:24, concludes, "For this reason a man will leave his father and mother and be united to his wife, and they will become one flesh." The Lord created us so that men and women do not hold onto their parents for their whole life. A time comes when we all desire to leave the family bond in order to begin a new bond in marriage. While the connection with our first family will continue to be important after marriage, it is no longer the primary bond. The intense desire between a man and woman is the beginning of the move away from each of their families towards a new relationship in marriage. In this relationship, a man and woman only have eyes for one another, and they do not have thoughts or desires for other men or other women. If you are in a relationship and your mind wanders to others, then you are not ready to make a commitment in that relationship. If you still have doubts about the man you are thinking about marrying, or find that you do not care if he is with you or not, then you need to ask yourself whether you are actually ready for marriage.

Here again, the image of our relationship with Jesus Christ gives us direction. Since we are the bride of Christ we are to be so preoccupied with him that we can say, like the words of this song, he is like a sachet of myrrh resting between our breasts, a constant fragrance that covers our whole life. A living relationship with Jesus Christ does not just involve remembering him during times of special devotions but this relationship is experienced in a deeply rooted desire for the Lord Jesus every single day of our life. He must constantly be on our mind like a pleasant aroma that always surrounds us. Then we will constantly be thinking about how our actions are going to impact our relationship with him. We want to honour the Lord Jesus in everything we do, and we want all our actions to bring glory to his name.

Even after years of marriage, a husband and wife who truly love one another will keep each other on their mind throughout the day. In the many decisions that need to be made during the day, each will always take into account the well-being of their spouse. For example, if you are delayed at work at the end of the day, you will instantly think of your wife, because you know she will worry if you are not home at the regular time, so you will call or text her to let her know what is happening. And when you need to make a decision about something, immediately you will take into account the impact it will have on your spouse. The man or woman on whom you have set your heart will always be on your mind, but in a good way. It should not be an obsessive kind of attention that can become unhealthy as you try to control each other. Within a healthy relationship you will give each other freedom while you also constantly watch out for each other's needs. And once you are married, as a wife you want the world to see that you are a loving bride, and as a husband you want the world to see that you love your wife by caring for her. In this way you bring honour on each other.

A love that refreshes

After telling us that her beloved is constantly on her mind, the woman in this song expresses how his love refreshes and renews her. In 1:14 she declares, "My lover is to me a cluster of henna blossoms from the vineyard of En Gedi." En Gedi is an oasis on the western shore of the Dead Sea.[5] The area is desolate and difficult to travel through, so coming across this oasis with its waterfall would be a wonderful discovery. In the middle of the barren land, the green grass, trees and vines of the oasis are a welcome sight because here the traveller finds wonderful refreshment. This oasis is a source of life.

This woman compares her beloved to this well-known oasis that served as an invigorating retreat. Just like the weary traveller found refreshment at the oasis, she finds refreshment with him. For her, he is like the loveliest flower in this oasis, one that reminds her of his perfume again. The henna blossom is small but highly prized for its beauty and fragrance and sought after for perfumes and cosmetics. This is a wonderful image with which she tells her beloved how special he is to her. That openness and joyful expression of love is the way we should speak and behave towards each other in our relationships.

It is fair to wonder if the love depicted in this song is being idealized. Is it really possible for any man or woman to experience such an intense and loving feeling for each other? I am sure that those who are married will say that it is not always this way in marriage. There are times when we do not have romantic thoughts about our spouse, when we do not carry them around like a sachet of myrrh between our breasts and when we do not think of them as an oasis where we find refreshment. There are many times that the intensity we felt in our courtship is missing in our marriage. How is it possible to maintain these things in a marriage? Many books have been written to help couples keep the intimacy in their relationship alive. They may give many helpful suggestions about maintaining your love life, but they do not actually address the real issue. The key to a meaningful marriage as God intended it rests in your relationship with Jesus Christ. Without a living relationship with Christ who gave his life for his bride, you do not have a strong foundation on which to build your marriage. If Jesus Christ is not the oasis in whom you find your spiritual refreshment, then how can you love each other as Christ loved you? When Christ is a constant presence in your thoughts and a constant fragrant aroma in your life, your love for each other will be reinvigorated each day.

It should be clear that when men do not turn to Christ daily for spiritual nourishment, they will be relying on their own strength in their attempt to give loving leadership to their wife as well as tender love and care for her in every situation. And if wives do not find their refreshment in Christ, they will not find the strength to show loving respect to their husband in every situation or to look to him for refreshment in their time of need. And if you as a young couple do not base your courtship on Jesus Christ as your Lord, then where will you find strength to maintain your love for each other once the first rush of love is gone? Putting Christ first in your life will also put him first in your courtship. And if as a couple you put Christ first, then in him you will be able to sing the marvelous words of this love song together for the rest of your life.

For Further Reflection

1. What message does the man convey to his beloved when he compares her to a mare among Pharaoh's chariots? How do you convey a similar message to the one you love?

2. Discuss the appropriateness of a man using the imagery of jewellery to describe his love and the message he conveys to her by doing this. What are the qualities that truly make a woman beautiful?

3. Discuss why it is important for a man to speak to his beloved about his love and care for her.

4. If a woman is to "put on" inner beauty, what is the value of the man adorning his beloved with jewellery? How does this practice reflect Christ's dealings with his bride, the church? How does he adorn her?

5. How does a man create a comfortable and secure environment for his beloved to flourish?

6. The woman calls her beloved her king. Discuss what this reveals about the attitude of the woman to her beloved and how this is important for the relationship. How does this attitude relate to our relationship with Jesus Christ?

7. What feeling does the woman convey when she speaks about her beloved as a sachet of myrrh resting between her breasts? What does this teach about the progression of love in a relationship in light of Genesis 2:24? What implications does this have for our relationship with Jesus Christ?

8. Discuss how the image of En Gedi (an oasis) represents a sense of refreshment for the couple. How should the love experienced by a man and woman become a source of refreshment in their life?

9. Do you think the love depicted in this song is being idealized? Is it possible to experience such love in one's relationship? How does Christ have a role in developing such a relationship in your life?

Chapter 4

Becoming One

Man

> How beautiful you are, my darling!
> Oh, how beautiful!
> Your eyes are doves.

Woman

> How handsome you are, my beloved!
> Oh, how charming!

Together

> And our bed is verdant.
> The beams of our house are cedars;
> our rafters are firs.

Woman

> I am a rose of Sharon,
> a lily of the valleys.

Man

> Like a lily among thorns
> is my darling among the young women.

Woman

> Like an apple tree among the trees of the forest
> is my beloved among the young men.
> I delight to sit in his shade,
> and his fruit is sweet to my taste.
> Let him lead me to the banquet hall,

and let his banner over me be love.
Strengthen me with raisins,
refresh me with apples,
for I am faint with love.
His left arm is under my head,
and his right arm embraces me.
Daughters of Jerusalem, I charge you
by the gazelles and by the does of the field:
Do not arouse or awaken love
until it so desires."
(Song of Songs 1:15–2:7)

A good relationship is never static but continually grows. Although the poet of this song does not intend to give us a storyline, the poetry makes us aware of changes in the relationship. As this couple speaks to each other, we become aware of the movement in their thoughts and emotions. Here, two individuals begin to think in terms of becoming one and speak as if they hold all things in common. Their lives are becoming so entwined that they begin to feel a common bond. They begin to desire marriage so that they may consummate their love and live together in their own home.

Love sees all things in common

The poetry of 1:15–17 suggests that the couple have gone for a walk into the forest. Walking together in the woods gives them the opportunity to talk about what lives in their hearts. From their talk, it is clear that their relationship has progressed to the point at which they are able to express their deepest thoughts and feelings for each other. Being smitten with love for her, this man speaks to the heart of the one he loves in 1:15, "How beautiful you are, my darling! Oh, how beautiful! Your eyes are doves."

In our culture, the expression "your eyes are doves" does not stir up any romantic feelings, but it must have had a romantic ring in their culture, or at least between the two of them. In the ancient Near East, doves were often used as a symbol for love. Many stone engravings from that period depict a man and woman in a romantic setting with a dove flying either between them or above them. Therefore the expression "your eyes are doves" must convey some kind of romantic feeling. In any case, from his words she immediately recognizes and understands that her eyes attract him. Sometimes people speak about how they were first attracted to their spouse because of their eyes. This man loves to gaze into her eyes that are so beautiful to him. It's as if he could gaze right into her soul. Her eyes melt his heart. The woman responds in kind, saying, "How handsome you are, my beloved! Oh, how charming!" Notice how openly and unashamedly she speaks about her admiration of him.

This song demonstrates that it is very natural for a man and woman to speak in glowing terms about each other. That does not mean that they are not aware of each other's shortcomings, for true love should not make us blind to each other's weaknesses. Instead, genuine love is patient and kind and will not let those weaknesses destroy the relationship. Such genuine love is only possible when our relationship grows in the love of Christ. We love someone in the way God intended within a relationship when we understand how Christ first revealed his love for us. Christ is patient and kind and long-suffering toward us. He even gave his life for us to pay for our sins and shortcomings. Knowing how much the Lord has forgiven us gives us the motivation to forgive the sins committed against each other. Only on the basis of Christ's love for us will we be able to grow in that kind of love for someone else. With this couple, each shows a genuine respect and love for the other that forms the basis for the glowing words they speak to each another.

Often when someone showers us with words of praise we find it difficult to accept that praise. We may feel that we are not worthy of such praise and question whether the words are genuine. A woman may feel that she is not that beautiful, especially when she compares herself to the beautiful girls on the covers of fashion magazines. When couples express their love for each other in such glowing terms, they are not saying that the other person meets society's standards of beauty, but they are saying, "You are the most important person in my life. You are the one I love. To me, you are the most beautiful woman or you are the most handsome man in the world." When you understand that these are genuine words spoken from the heart, then you will also accept them in that way and it will give you confidence in your relationship.

Verse 17 of this first chapter of the song indicates another development in the relationship. The couple are walking together and talking, and at a certain point they look around and say to each other, "And our bed is verdant. The beams of our house are cedars; our rafters are firs." They must have come to a place in their walk where they are surrounded by lush green growth, with a rich patch of green grass underfoot and a green canopy of leaves above. There are cedar trees surrounding them like a wall for protection, and fir trees that form a roof give a beautiful canopy of greenery above them. This setting in the forest is a beautiful, protected place that makes them think of a house that could be theirs, and they refer to the lush grass as their bed. This is the most beautiful place they can imagine and they want to call it their home. Being together in this beautiful place seems to them to be the closest thing they will ever find to paradise on earth.

Notice the development from the use of "you" and "me" to "our" in verses 15–17. In these verses, they have moved from describing each other as individuals and praising each other's beauty to speaking about the things that they have together. They already dream about the verdant bed and the house made of cedars that will be "ours." In every relationship, there is a time when two individuals begin to see themselves as one and to think in terms of "us." This is a subtle change that couples often do not even notice at first, but it is an important development in a relationship. This beautiful place makes them think of a wonderful home, and they begin to long in their heart for the day when they will have their own home.

Love delights only in each other

The next verses give us a sense that this couple is becoming more confident in their relationship as they indicate their delight in one another. The woman expresses that confidence when she says in 2:1, "I am a rose of Sharon, a lily of the valleys." While Sharon is the fertile coastal plain located south of Mount Carmel along the Mediterranean Sea, there is uncertainty about the identity of the flowers to which she compares herself.[1] Commentators argue among themselves about whether this woman is comparing herself to a very valuable flower or to a common flower. If she compares herself to a flower that was highly prized at that time then she thinks very highly of herself, but if she compares herself to a common flower, then she reveals a humble spirit.[2] It seems to me the point is simply that she compares herself to a beautiful flower. She is not necessarily exalting herself as the most beautiful flower in the world and neither is she putting herself down by saying she is just a lowly flower. She has enough confidence in herself to describe herself in this way, and she knows herself to be attractive to the man who loves her. Here she shows how she has grown in her self-image. Earlier, in 1:6, she said to the daughters of Jerusalem, "Do not stare at me because I am dark, because I am darkened by the sun." At that point she was self-conscious about her appearance but now she describes herself in a more flattering way. What caused this change in her self-esteem? As their relationship developed, she began to look at herself through the eyes of this man. Her self-image has grown because she now sees herself as this man sees her.

For men, including husbands, telling the woman in your life that you love her and that she is beautiful will give her confidence, causing her to become even more beautiful. This will happen because she becomes confident in her heart that you really care for her. This is God's plan for love. The Lord has created a man and woman in such a way that we have the ability to build each other up. Therefore, never underestimate the influence you have on your spouse, both for good when you encourage her and for bad when you do not. The man of this song responds to the woman in 2:2: "Like a lily among the thorns, is my darling among the maidens." He takes what she has just said about the flowers and adds that she is not just a rose among roses or a lily among lilies but that she stands out like a lily among the thorns. In his eyes, she is different from all the other girls and he only has eyes for her. The other girls seem ordinary in comparison to the one on whom he has set his heart.

As I wrote these words, a young couple walked by the window of my study on their way home from school. It was obvious that they were fighting and since they did not notice me sitting behind my desk, they carried on their argument. This girl was very angry with the young man because he had been looking at and made some inappropriate comments about some girls they had walked by. She was angry because he did not have eyes only for her. As he tried to make up by kissing her, she refused, saying that his kisses were not going to make it better. This young woman did not feel confident in the love of her young man because it was clear that he did not see her as a lily among thorns. His attitude was quite different from that of the man in this song.

As we listen to this couple in the song speak about their love for each other, it directs our thoughts to the relationship that we have with Christ. A fundamental principle in this relationship is that *the way you look at yourself will be determined by the way you listen to Jesus Christ.* God's children often wonder about the love of Christ for them; for example, how can the Lord love me when I am so sinful? Or when I look at my life and I see that I have accomplished so little, I don't feel worthy of his love. Thinking this way, we end up despising ourselves, because we know ourselves very well and are ashamed of our sins and shortcomings. Instead, the woman of the song looks at herself through the eyes of the man and finds confidence. In the same way, we need to look at ourselves through the eyes of Jesus Christ. When Jesus Christ speaks to his bride, the church, he speaks about his great love and care for her. He speaks to her heart about how beautiful she is in his eyes. But, you ask, how can the Lord speak such words of endearment and love to me? How can he say to me how beautiful I am in his eyes if he knows my dark secret? We know we are all sinners who have rebelled against God and done things that we are ashamed of. Christ knows this too, but he says, "You are mine and to me you are the most beautiful person in the whole world for you are the apple of my eye" (Deuteronomy 32:10; Zechariah 2:8).

The Lord Jesus speaks in that way because he has entered into a covenant relationship with his people. He is the one who washes away all the dirt of sin, who removes our shame with his blood and who clothes us with new, white and spotless wedding garments. He is the one who adorns us with earrings and necklaces of gold. Our Saviour comes and speaks about his love for us. So when you look at yourself, you must do so through the eyes of the great bridegroom, Jesus Christ. He gives you wonderful encouragement. But if you do not believe that you are washed in his blood and if you do not listen in faith to his words of endearment and love for you, how can you ever have any confidence in your life? There is no reason for any of God's covenant children to doubt the words of the Saviour. When he tells you about his love and he speaks about your beauty, a beauty that he has given to you through his shed blood on the cross, then you may feel secure in his love. On the other hand, if you do not enjoy the security of Christ, it may very well be that you are refusing to trust and believe in him. If you do not accept that his words of love are true and genuine, you are refusing to live in an intimate relationship with Jesus Christ. But by seeing yourself as Christ now sees you, redeemed in his blood, you can indeed say that in Christ, I have become a beautiful rose of Sharon, a lily of the valley.

After the man speaks about his delight in his beloved, the woman confidently responds in 2:3, declaring her delight in the man she loves: "Like an apple tree among the trees of the forest is my lover among the young men. I delight to sit in his shade, and his fruit is sweet to my taste." An apple tree stands out from all the other trees because of the enticing fruit hanging from its branches. People are immediately drawn to its fruit. This woman tells her beloved that in her eyes he stands out among the other young men like an apple tree stands out among the other trees. Her greatest delight is to be able to sit in his shade. In Psalm 1, the godly man is compared to a tree that when planted by the streams of water yields its fruit in season. She sees in this man someone who yields the wonderful fruit of righteousness. Earlier, she spoke about working in her parent's vineyard in the heat of the sun so that her complexion has become dark (1:6). Now she looks at this man as her protector and one in whose shade she finds relief and rest. Not only does he act as a shade over her but he is a tree offering fruit that is sweet to the taste and, oh, so refreshing. This is a man who is worthy of her love.

As a woman in a relationship, you must also ask yourself whether the man you love is a man that you can respect. Do you delight to sit in his shade? Is he the kind of man that you can trust to protect you? If he does not make you feel safe and secure—if you are always on edge, not knowing what he will do at any moment—then he is not the man for you. You must be sure that the man you love is strong in faith and loves to serve the Lord. He must be a man who will always stand beside you, encouraging you in your service of the Lord. If you cannot depend on him to encourage you to serve God, then you can't be sure that he will be your shade to protect you and that he will provide fruit that is sweet to your taste.

The wonderful security that this woman feels in the love of this man is expressed in 2:4: "He has taken me to the banquet hall, and his banner over me is love." In an army a banner could be the flag identifying a regiment and carried by one of the soldiers into battle. In a marching band a banner is used to identify it in a parade. In these cases and more generally as well a banner identifies who you belong to.[3] Like a banner, this man's love for her is clear for everyone to see. His love is not only something he talks about to her in private, but he is proud to show everyone in the world that this girl is very special to him. When they go to the banquet hall, which is a public place, he does not ignore her but he makes their special relationship clear to everyone.[4] This kind of open declaration of his love without any embarrassment would make a woman feel very secure. It is also a model for how husbands should speak about their wives to others. It is very easy to fall into complaining or making derogatory remarks about your spouse, but that is not holding a banner of love over her. When you do not clearly convey your love and respect for your wife to others, even when she is not present, you are undermining your relationship.

Jesus Christ is also a model for a husband's banner of love. Christ loved his church to the point of self-sacrifice, providing for her physical, emotional and spiritual needs. He always leads with love and compassion and never with tyranny. By putting his mark or banner on us, he says to the whole world, "I claim this person for my own for I have bought him or her with my blood." His banner over you means that you can rest secure in the love of your Saviour. He is the one who gave his life for your life. Our greatest sense of peace and security is that we can live in the love of our Lord.

Love desires consummation

Love between a man and a woman is a very powerful emotion, and as the woman continues to speak, her words reveal that her emotions are overwhelmed. She says in verse 5, "I am faint with love," or more literally, "I am sick with love." She asks her beloved, "Strengthen me with raisins, refresh me with apples." Apples and raisins might be considered aphrodisiacs and included here to heighten the sense of love and emotion that is being felt by the woman. But in this context, the woman does not seem to be in need of an aphrodisiac but rather of physical sustenance. Her overwhelming emotions leave her feeling weak. Therefore, she asks the man to strengthen her with raisins and refresh her with apples, for she is faint with love.

Her next words in 2:6, "His left arm is under my head, and his right arm embraces me," describe the posture of a couple who are physically intimate with one another. She longs to be held in the secure and loving embrace of the one she loves,[5] and she longs for the day when their relationship is consummated in the most intimate way. It is perfectly natural for a man and woman in love to feel such attraction. If that is not the case, there is something drastically wrong in the relationship. The strong physical attraction between a man and a woman are part of God's design for developing relationships. But God, through this song, also indicates how he wants these desires to be dealt with. Just because a couple feel such a desire for each other does not mean that unmarried couples have a license to act on them. God's instruction about this is found in the woman's warning, "Daughters of Jerusalem, I charge you by the gazelles and by the does of the field: Do not arouse or awaken love until it so desires." At this moment, the woman of this song is asking the daughters of Jerusalem to swear an oath in which there are sexual connotations. Within the Canaanite cultural context, her reference to gazelles and deer would almost certainly indicate sexual undertones since Canaanite art discovered from that time depicts these animals within sexual contexts. The Song of Songs itself refers to the woman's breasts being "like two fawns, twins of a gazelle." These Israelite maidens would have been aware of these sexual elements within the oath.

It is possible that she could just be warning these girls, who also want to experience love, not to force it but instead just to wait for love to blossom, and not to hurry it.[6] From the preceding verses of the song, however, it is clear that the woman has come to the point of experiencing intense sexual longing for the man she loves, and because of that she warns, "Do not arouse or awaken love until it so desires." The words "arouse" and "awaken" come from the same root word, and this repetition adds a sense of urgency to her warning. She is not simply suggesting that these girls avoid a love relationship until they are ready for it; she is warning them not to toy with their sexual desires. Her own situation has made her aware of the dangers and difficulties of this. She wants to make a pact with these girls that they will not give in to their sexual desires before the proper time. These could be friends making a promise to each other that they will keep themselves pure until their wedding day and that they will hold one another accountable to that promise.

This woman's advice that they should not force the development of love, or not try to awaken it until it desires, was counsel that she needed for herself at this time. She was being overwhelmed by her own desire to consummate the relationship. She feels intense longing, but she must be patient for the time when the Lord will fulfill her desire on the wedding day. This advice is still very relevant for couples today. As your relationship develops, there will be a growing desire to consummate your love. While the desire is natural, you have to be patient and wait for the appropriate time, which the Lord will give you. The woman's advice, "not to arouse or awaken love," refers to the reality that dating couples need to learn to contain the fire of their passion. If that desire is not contained, there will be damaging consequences for the relationship. Love can be compared to a fire in the fireplace of a living room. As long as the fire is contained to the fireplace it is a wonderful source of heat for the home, but when it is allowed escape the boundaries of the fireplace it will burn up the whole house. Sexual passion that is not contained will damage your relationship. When you express yourself sexually before marriage, the message you give your partner is not necessarily one of love. Even if both parties consent equally to the act, it is an action based on physical need and not one that shows proper respect for each other.

It invites a number of destructive elements into your still growing relationship: you might feel used, your self-esteem or self-confidence might be damaged and you might feel guilty or insecure. None of these are helpful to a relationship. Your relationship cannot grow and flourish when you have to deal with guilt in your heart.

After marriage, the situation is different. Marriage brings a tremendous freedom, because you can express your love to each other in the most intimate way within the security you feel in your marriage bond, and there is no sense of guilt. It is important to understand that outside of marriage, sex becomes something that consumes us. It is preoccupying and demands constant gratification, and this gets more and more difficult to attain. A relationship based on illicit sex will burn itself out since it is not part of a properly developed relationship. In marriage, however, the sexual relationship is not in the first place about gratification; rather, it is about intimately expressing your love for each other as a husband and wife. The sexual relationship does not define the bond, but instead it is something that enhances it. What maintains the relationship in marriage is a growing respect and tenderness for each other and a mutual desire to work together for the Lord. The period of courtship must, therefore, be a time of restraint when desire is kept within proper boundaries. To enjoy God's blessing in your relationship, you must not let your hormones control your actions. It is much easier to let our desires rule us, but when you let this happen the desires will run rampant in your life and in the end cause you pain. By waiting, you allow your wedding day to be a truly special day of freedom and wondrous joy when you may express your desire in the most intimate way.

A couple in love longs for the day when their relationship will be consummated, and there is a parallel desire in the heart of God's people for the consummation that will take place at the great wedding feast. Just as the woman of the song longs for the day when she can lie in the embrace of her beloved, so God's people today long for the day they may forever live in the embrace of their Saviour. The great marriage feast will be a wonderful occasion when we will be united with our Lord in the most glorious way. That day is not here yet, and in the meantime we need to be patient and prepare ourselves. The apostle John, in a vision in Revelation 19:7, looks into the future when the wedding feast has come and observes, "The bride has made herself ready." The bride as the church prepares herself for that day by living a holy and sanctified life. It is her desire to put away the sin that still clings to her and to live a life holy and pleasing to her Lord.

For Further Reflection

1. It is important for couples to express their love and care for each other. Since each spouse has his or her own sins and weaknesses, how is it possible for husbands and wives to continue to express appreciation and love for each other? What qualities does Christ's love for us have that should be reflected in our marriage?

2. Why do people often find it difficult to accept words of praise? Under what conditions will such words of praise be accepted? Why is it important that spouses learn to praise each other and how will doing this reflect Christ's relationship with his people?

3. How has the relationship developed as the couple walks through the verdant forest and dream about their home? Discuss how this is being reflected in your relationship.

4. What does the woman's comparison of herself to a beautiful flower say about her self-image? What contributed to the development of her self-esteem? Discuss how you will help build each other's self-esteem so love may flourish in your relationship.

5. Discuss the principle: the way you look at yourself will be determined by the way you listen to Jesus Christ.

6. What does the woman mean when she compares her beloved to an apple tree in the forest and says she delights to sit in the shade of his tree? What does this teach men about the character they need to develop for their own lives?

7. What is the security the woman feels when she speaks about her beloved taking her to the banquet hall and says that his banner over her is love? Discuss the banner Christ places over us and the sense of security it gives.

8. Why is it necessary for dating couples to contain their passion? What are some consequences if the woman's warning is not heeded?

9. How is a sexual relationship outside of marriage different from one experienced by a married couple? Why is the one healthy and not the other?

10. As the bride of Christ, how do we prepare ourselves for the great consummation when the bridegroom, Jesus Christ, will return?

Chapter 5

Love Bursts Forth Like Spring

Listen! My beloved!
Look! Here he comes,
leaping across the mountains,
bounding over the hills.
My beloved is like a gazelle or a young stag.
Look! There he stands behind our wall,
gazing through the windows,
peering through the lattice.
My beloved spoke and said to me,

"Arise, my darling,
my beautiful one, come with me.
See! The winter is past;
the rains are over and gone.
Flowers appear on the earth;
the season of singing has come,
the cooing of doves is heard in our land.
The fig tree forms its early fruit;
the blossoming vines spread their fragrance.
Arise, come, my darling;
my beautiful one, come with me."
My dove in the clefts of the rock,
in the hiding places on the mountainside,

show me your face,
let me hear your voice;
for your voice is sweet,
and your face is lovely.

Catch for us the foxes,
the little foxes
that ruin the vineyards,
our vineyards that are in bloom.
My beloved is mine and I am his;
he browses among the lilies.
Until the day breaks
and the shadows flee,
turn, my beloved,
and be like a gazelle
or like a young stag
on the rugged hills.
(Song of Songs 2:8–17)

The previous chapter ended with the couple longing to consummate their relationship and the woman then warning the daughters of Jerusalem not to arouse or awaken love until the time is right. This warning marks a break in the song and the start of a new unit. In 2:6 the woman longed to be in the embrace of the man she loves, but in 2:8 there suddenly is a new perspective. Drawn to her window by something she hears, the woman now sees the man off in the distance coming toward her. This sudden shift is a clear signal that the song will now describe the couple's relationship from a different perspective. Within this new unit, the new love between the man and woman is described in terms of springtime, when new life begins to burst forth. Their blossoming love draws the couple closer and they want to know even more about one another, and the more they get to know each other the more they desire a commitment from each other.

Love seeks knowledge

The woman is drawn to her window first by something she hears. "Listen! My beloved!" she exclaims in 2:8. But then she sees him coming: "Look! Here he comes, leaping across the mountains, bounding over the hills." You can hear the excitement in her voice as she hears and then sees the man bounding toward her home. Every woman in love today knows this feeling. You keep your phone very close and you constantly check for messages or wait for it to ring, because you want to hear from the man you love. Just a few months earlier, before the relationship began, the sound of a text message wasn't quite so thrilling; it would just be a text from the same old friends. That is what love does. It brings a new interest and excitement into your life.

The description the woman gives of the man coming toward her house expresses something of how he must feel about her. Watching him leaping and bounding toward her home, he appears to her to be like a gazelle or young stag. Gazelles are small, fast antelope that run gracefully and a stag is a male deer; together they invoke an image of strength and grace. She admires how effortlessly he runs and leaps down the path to her home. Any mother of a grown son reading this will smile and remember how hard it was to get her son to run an errand. I remember how frustrated my mother was asking any one of her five sons to go somewhere for her. They complained that they were too tired after a hard day at work or too busy with something else. The man in this song may have walked this path many times before, probably just trudging along because it is hard work to walk up and down those hills so often. But now, in love, he runs effortlessly and with seemingly limitless energy. When a man falls in love, it is never too far, too tiring or too much to go visit that special girl. That is the way love works, and that is the kind of change it brings in a man.

This man now bounds up to her house, but when he arrives, he stops and stands outside of the wall. "Look!" she says. "There he stands behind our wall, gazing through the windows, peering through the lattice." This courtship has not yet progressed to the point where he is free to enter her home. He waits outside, hoping that she will come out and see him. But in the meantime, he gazes at the window and peeks through the lattice to see if he can get a glimpse of the one he loves. There is some tension here as the man waits, wanting to see his love and wondering, as we are, if she will come out to see him.

But the woman does come out to speak with him, and she reports: "My beloved spoke and said to me, 'Arise, my darling, my beautiful one, and come with me.'" His words begin and end with a command, but in between he praises her and seduces her by calling her "my darling" and describing her as "my beautiful one." He has set his heart on her and his urgent words sound like a command for her to come away with him. His words remind us of how at the beginning of the song, in 1:4, it was the woman who spoke urgent words, commanding the man to take her away. Now it is he who commands her to come away with him. He also gives her a reason to come with him and explains the urgency of his longing. It is springtime and he wants her to come out and enjoy it with him. His own description of spring in 2:11 tells us what it means to him: "See! The winter is past; the rains are over and gone. Flowers appear on the earth; the season of singing has come, the cooing of doves is heard in our land. The fig tree forms its early fruit; the blossoming vines spread their fragrance." Winter is over and he is seeing everything coming to life around him.

Spring throughout the generations and across cultures is a symbol of love. Over the centuries, much love poetry that has been written is filled with the imagery of spring. When people fall in love, it is as if spring has come into their hearts. New love is like the flowers that begin to peek out and then spring up from the ground to brighten the earth after the drabness of winter. In the springtime, the mating call of the doves can be heard again as they coo to one another. Spring is about new life and the renewal of life. When people fall in love, to them it is as if they are experiencing a new life. Suddenly, their perspective changes and their lives take on a whole new meaning. Before a man meets the girl of his dreams, he might be bored or lacking in motivation, but now suddenly he is alert, full of enthusiasm and active. Love has that kind of effect on people, giving them a new purpose and focus in life.

The fact that love can bring about such a change in people is not so strange when you consider how your relationship with Jesus

Christ brings change into your life. The Lord Jesus comes as the great bridegroom who has given his life for us, and his love for us brings renewal into our lives. He comes with his gospel and urgently calls us to arise and come away with him, and we are filled with the greatest joy that we will ever experience. There is no greater joy than to know the great love of Jesus Christ for us. The love of Christ changes our whole perspective on life. Without Christ, life can be compared to the winter, a time when it is dreary, dull and uncomfortable, and there is no life on the trees or the ground. When you experience the love of Christ in your life, on the other hand, it is like winter has turned to spring. There is newness in your life, as you feel a renewed purpose and vigour. With Christ, life is worth living because you are able to enjoy the protecting love of your Saviour. In this way, the song speaks to everyone, and not just to couples experiencing a human love relationship. The image of Christ as the one who brings spring into our lives points to the fact that everyone—young, old, married, widowed or single—can experience real joy and happiness. Paul made it clear that fulfillment and purpose in this life does not depend on marriage. He found his greatest fulfillment in his relationship with Jesus Christ, and his greatest joy was to be busy with Christ's work in the kingdom of God (see 1 Corinthians 7:32–35).

For Christian couples, the experience of true love awakening in their hearts for someone else is only possible if they first know the love of Christ that awakens like spring in their own heart. When you experience love, as the couple of the song does, suddenly you will find a new sense of purpose within you. Now you have someone with whom you can share everything and about whom you want to know everything. These feelings cause the man to call out in 2:14, "My dove in the clefts of the rock, in the hiding places on the mountainside, show me your face, let me hear your voice; for your voice is sweet, and your face is lovely." He is still calling the woman to come out with him. Again, there is a reference to a dove in his words, an ancient Near Eastern symbol of love, as he calls out to her. But his dove is hiding from him. Doves live in the crevices of the rock and in hiding places in the cliffs. The "mountainside" in 2:14 literally means steep places and probably refers to the cliffs where the doves live. The man is calling her out of her hiding place, asking her to come out and show him her face. His words could be understood in a broader sense as well, where he is really saying that he wants her to come out of her hiding place and let him know everything there is to know about her. He wants to understand what is living in her heart and to know her opinions about things. He wants her to tell him what she feels, because he wants to know what she likes and dislikes. He wants to know her aspirations in life, her dreams and plans. He calls her to come out so that he can learn about her and get to know her intimately.

Here we have an important principle for every relationship. Couples need to take the time to study one another so that they get to know everything about each other. This is important for a healthy relationship and a reason why the physical and sexual element in the relationship must wait. I am not only referring to overt sexual intimacy here, but I am convinced that no relationship should immediately proceed to passionate touching and kissing either. A focus on the physical passion detracts from the more important element of getting to know one another. Your relationship can only develop in a meaningful way when you first take the time to know each other, because the better you understand each other, the better you can also serve each other. This is a principle that is true for married couples as well, as they need to continue to study each other their whole married life, for you can never say that you know everything about your husband or your wife. Your marriage relationship needs to keep growing, and that is only possible through a lifetime of studying each other. As the circumstances and stages of our lives change, our thinking changes and develops, our tastes change and our needs change. The more a couple understands and knows each other, the better you can love and serve each other. The same principle is true for your relationship with Jesus Christ. We are called to study Christ and all he has done for us. Through the word of God we come to know the greatness of our bridegroom, Jesus Christ. The more we know and understand the redeeming work of Jesus Christ for us, the better we will be able to love and serve him with our whole life.

The man continues in 2:14 and expresses how he wants to hear the voice of the girl he loves, as it is like sweet music to his ears. He could listen to her voice all day long and never grow weary of it. The poet touches on the fact that it is important to listen to your beloved as a part of knowing them. God created man and woman so that they are able to commune together at the deepest level. It is God's purpose that a man and woman should live together with the most intimate knowledge of each other. A husband and wife should never need to hide anything from each other, because they are to be one, not only physically but also spiritually and emotionally. They are to share everything so that they can work together in the most intimate way. That is God's intention for marriage (Genesis 2:18–25).

The oneness and unity of a married couple must begin to develop during courtship. Getting to know each other takes time and cannot be rushed, so couples should never shorten their time of courtship and be in a hurry to get married. You need to give yourself time to build trust, and as you slowly build trust you will also begin to share more and more about yourself with the one you love. And that will not be possible either if you are always busy with all kinds of activities, never leaving time to talk together about important matters in your life. Above all else, it is your relationship with Christ that is the most important matter you need to talk about together. One of the most important things for a couple is to read God's Word and pray together. Through this spiritual activity you will truly grow in your relationship and you will begin to form a vision together for the future that will be based on your relationship with Christ. Engaging in a sexual relationship before you are married will make it impossible for your own relationship as well as your spiritual relationship with the Lord to grow because of the guilt it brings into your life.

The development of your relationship as a couple should then be a reflection of the unfolding of your relationship with Christ. Just as you love to learn more about each other, you must love to learn more about Jesus Christ as your bridegroom. It is impossible to grow in your relationship with Christ if you do not learn more about him, and in the same way it is impossible to grow in your relationship with a man or woman, and for that matter with your husband or wife, if you are not constantly learning more about each other. Growing in love will lead to a lifetime of faithful commitment to each other.

Love seeks commitment

The woman responds to the man's call in 2:15–17, and her main thought is found in verse 16: "My beloved is mine and I am his." Her choice of words implies that they make a claim on each other. Her response to his call for her to come out with him makes it clear that she does not want to enter into an open-ended relationship. She wants a relationship in which they make a firm commitment to each other. Today, many will say that this is an old-fashioned idea, but the greatest joy for this couple is that they *own* each other. In effect she is saying, "I claim ownership of you and I am giving myself to you." Love can never be open-ended, and as you begin to travel down the road of love you have to make a decision; there will be a point when you either realize that you do not want to commit yourself to the relationship or that you are ready to give yourself to it for the rest of your life.

In the culture of today there is the opinion that marriage is an old and outdated institution that can no longer function in our modern society. There appears to be some justification for this thought as Statistics Canada predicts that about forty per cent of all marriages will end in failure. But why do marriages end in failure? Part of the reason might be that many think of marriage as an open-ended relationship. Couples enter marriage with the romantic notion that it will last a lifetime, but at the same time they are ready to give up on the marriage when it no longer serves their purpose or when the going becomes difficult. The couple in this song, however, expresses that they are fully committed to each other when she says, "My beloved is mine and I am his."

This development in the relationship is also patterned on the relationship that we have with Jesus Christ. Generations of believers have confessed with the words of the Heidelberg Catechism, Lord's Day 1, "That I am not my own, but belong with body and soul, both in life and death, to my faithful Saviour Jesus Christ." This wonderful confession gives great comfort. Do you ever think about what this means? Do you really know what you are confessing? As a believer, I am confessing that Jesus Christ is mine for he belongs to me and that I am his. My greatest comfort is that I am wholly the possession of my Saviour, Jesus Christ. I am in a committed relationship with Jesus that will stand for eternity. It is in his arms that I have life and salvation and in whom I am fully secure. That relationship with Christ must be reflected in your marriage relationship.

When you make a commitment to marriage, your greatest joy is to say to your spouse, "My beloved is mine and I am his." It is the reason that Paul can say in 1 Corinthians 7:4 that the wife's body belongs to the husband and the husband's body belongs to his wife. Once you have made a marriage commitment to each other, you can no longer hold anything back. In the same way, Christ gave himself for you, holding nothing back when he gave his own life for you on the cross, so your marriage should reflect this love. This is a commitment the couple of the song does not make reluctantly but with great joy. Love for each other has sprung to life and gives them a new purpose. Therefore, it is only natural that they desire to give themselves to one another for the rest of their lives.

And when you make such a commitment, you do not want anything to destroy it. The woman puts this into words when she says to the man in 2:15, "Catch for us the foxes, the little foxes that ruin the vineyards, our vineyards that are in bloom." She picks up the man's theme of verse 13 where he speaks about vineyards and blossoms. In the springtime the vineyards come into bloom, but spring is also a vulnerable time for the new growth because it is still tender and fragile and needs to be protected. The little foxes (this may refer to fox cubs) running through the vineyard are a threat to the new growth with its blooms. To protect the tender vines with the blossoms, the little foxes need to be caught as otherwise there will not be much of a harvest.

The vineyard is a metaphor for this couple's relationship. The woman's concern is for the small things that, left uncaught, threaten to do so much damage to their relationship. It is not the big things, or the big foxes, but the little things that threaten our relationships the most, and there are so many of them. The little things quickly add up and cause ruin. Some of these can be jealousy, differences of opinion and arguments about unimportant issues that you have let become important. The woman of the song is concerned about their relationship, because every relationship involves two sinners, each struggling with their own weaknesses and faults. The more you get to know each other, the more those weaknesses will become apparent. You are not looking for a perfect man or woman without sin and weaknesses. What this woman desires from her beloved is that they learn to deal with those little foxes in their relationship. If you do not learn how to deal with problems and differences in your time of courtship, then do not think for a moment everything will work out after you get married. Being able to work out your troubles in a proper way when you are dating is a sign that you will be able to deal with big problems after you are married. Couples need to assess how they handle their differences and arguments already before marriage. Disagreements themselves do not indicate a problem in the relationship, but there is a problem when a couple is never able to settle their arguments and differences. That pattern will continue in marriage and indicates that they are not ready to make a commitment to marriage. You must catch those little foxes before they become big problems, which means you must actively look for and deal with problems, and not run away from them with the hope they will go away on their own. Men tend to ignore problems, thinking that over time they will disappear. The reality is that our troubles will simply add up over time. This woman wisely counsels her beloved to catch the little foxes, for it is better to deal with the difficulties today in order to clear the air, not allowing anything in the relationship that may destroy it.

Now that a commitment has been made between the two in our song, there is a growing desire to enjoy the most intimate relationship. Her words in 2:16, "He browses among the lilies," can be read in a number of ways, perhaps referring to his lips as lilies since 5:13 describes them this way. But they could also be the woman's lips, upon which he is feeding. Regardless, it is clear that she is referring to an intimate act. She desires the most intimate relationship and appears already to be thinking about the wedding day when she says in verse 17, "Until the day breaks and the shadows flee, turn my beloved, and be like a gazelle or like a young stag on the rugged hills." Later, there is a description of the wedding night in 4:6 when the man responds to this invitation of the woman saying, "Until the day breaks and the shadows flee, I will go to the mountain of myrrh and to the hill of incense." On the wedding day he acts on the desire that is expressed by the woman in this text, but here she is already anticipating the wedding when they may freely express their love till the day breaks and the shadows of the night flee in the morning. A couple in a committed relationship yearns for the day when the Lord will let them express their love to one another in the fullest and most intimate way possible.

This yearning for the consummation between the two in the song reflects the yearning of God's people for the great bridegroom, Jesus Christ. Our life only has meaning and purpose within the context of our relationship with Jesus Christ. Jesus Christ who has made us his own, having bought us with his blood, is the one who will return from heaven in order to claim us for his very own. Therefore, if you know the love of Christ and you know that he has redeemed your life with his blood, then your heart will also long for the great day of his return. Then we will enter into an intimate living relationship with our Saviour that we cannot even begin to imagine today. When he returns he will remove all the little foxes from our life and bring us with him into the glorious life of God's kingdom. We eagerly look for our great bridegroom to return, leaping across mountains and bounding over hills so that we may forever be united with him in love.

For Further Reflection

1. Discuss how springtime is an appropriate metaphor for love.
2. How has the love of Christ brought renewal into your life?
3. Have you made an effort to study the one you love? Discuss how you can better understand each other and be more attentive to each other's needs.
4. Reflect on how effectively you study Christ and how you may improve your understanding of him. How important is it to you to know Christ and does that also reflect in the way you serve him?
5. Have you made it a habit in your courtship to read God's Word and pray together? How has this practice (or non-practice) affected your relationship?
6. Discuss some of the "little foxes" that threaten your marriage relationship and how you have dealt or will deal with them. What are some of the "little foxes" that negatively affect your relationship with Jesus Christ as your bridegroom?

Chapter 6

Longing for the One Her Heart Loves

All night long on my bed
I looked for the one my heart loves;
I looked for him but did not find him.
I will get up now and go about the city,
through its streets and squares;
I will search for the one my heart loves.
So I looked for him but did not find him.

The watchmen found me as they made their rounds in the city.
"Have you seen the one my heart loves?"

Scarcely had I passed them when I found the one my heart loves.
I held him and would not let him go
till I had brought him to my mother's house,
to the room of the one who conceived me.

Daughters of Jerusalem, I charge you
by the gazelles and by the does of the field:
Do not arouse or awaken love until it so desires.
(Song of Songs 3:1–5)

*I*t has already become clear that a growing and mature love relationship must be modelled on the love between God and his people, and no one can truly give or receive love if they do not first know the love of God in Christ Jesus. This song not only gives us a window into the love between a man and a woman but it also provides a window into understanding the love between God and his people—our relationship with the Lord. This second insight is revealed in the longing expressed by this woman. There are a number of things that stand out in her words in this section of the song. Four times she speaks about the man as "the one my heart loves," leaving no doubt about the depth of her love for him. We also discover three key words: *seek*, *found* and *held*. First the woman says that she will *seek* for this man, then that she *found* him and finally that she *held* on to him. She loves this man so much that she will search for him, and when she finds him she will not let go of him.

Seeking her beloved

We saw in 2:8–17 how the man came bounding across the hills to the woman's home to invite her to come out and enjoy the beauty of springtime. He wants her to come out so that he can study her and learn everything about her. As they learn more about each other, they grow in love. The end of chapter 2 of the song reveals the intensity of their love when the woman says, "My lover is mine and I am his; he browses among the lilies. Until the day breaks and the shadows flee, turn, my lover, and be like a gazelle or like a young stag on the rugged hills." She continues to speak passionately in the opening of this chapter: "All night long on my bed I looked for the one my heart loves; I looked for him but did not find him."

The scene has changed here, and now she is lying alone on her bed. As she lies on her bed at night she thinks about the one she loves and her deepest desire is that he might be with her. Some commentators are troubled by the imagery that is used in this section as some of it does not seem to fit the reality of life in Israel. For example, in those days it is doubtful that a woman would ever dare get up in the middle of the night and walk through the streets of the city on her own. It is helpful to keep in mind that poetry is not concerned about giving a real-life situation, because the purpose of poetry is to convey certain feelings. To do that, it will often leave out details about what is really happening or even present things in a way that might not make sense as a real-life situation. Rather than trying to read a realistic situation into this section, as many do, these words reflect instead the intense feeling of the woman when she says, "I looked for the one my heart loves; I looked for him but did not find him." The image here is not that this woman is actively searching around her room and through her whole house, as some suggest, but it instead conveys her mood as she lies on her bed and longs to be with the one she wants to have with her. This longing is not in the first place a sexual longing, although we should not deny that there is a sensual aspect to such longing. She speaks about a deep longing that love works in the hearts of two people who genuinely love each other.

Her words speak of a longing for "the one my soul loves." In Hebrew "the soul" refers to the life of a person. This word is used in Genesis 2:7 to describe how, when God breathed into the nostrils of the man, he caused the man to became a living being (soul); God's breath became the source of our life. It is the soul that animates us so that we are active and lively. The woman is telling us that to the very core of her being, right to the source of her life, her soul, she desires this man. That is what love does. Love is a very powerful emotion which causes us to want to give ourselves, our very soul, to another person.

Now, we also need to understand that ever since the fall into sin, this powerful emotion has the potential to be misused. The desires we feel are often desires for things that are evil, corrupt and even destructive. Sometimes, men and women set their heart on a person who is not good for them. The woman in the song has set her desire on a man who clearly displays godly virtues and has a good reputation. He is a man who has the same desire for the Lord that she has, and for that reason she sets her heart (soul) on this man. She knows that he is good for her, because he will care for her as the Lord cares for her. Often, however, we let our desires run in the wrong direction, giving our heart to the wrong boy or girl or to sinful and destructive desires. Paul in Romans 12:1, 2 urges the believer to follow things that are holy and good, saying, "In view of God's mercy, offer your bodies as living sacrifices, holy and pleasing to God—this is your true and proper worship." He warns, "Do not conform to the pattern of this world, but be transformed by the renewing of your mind." Paul reminds us that our passion, desire and delight should be for the Lord who has shown us is mercy. He warns us not to live according to the patterns of this world, which are sinful and destructive patterns. Quite naturally we deny God and use the powerful emotions we were created with, which the woman of the song expresses in these verses, in the pursuit of our own selfish desires. And when we set our hearts on our own selfish desires the result will be our own destruction. For that reason Paul urges us to channel our desires and passions in the right way; that is, in the ways of the Lord, so that we can expect to enjoy his blessings.

In our song, the woman now desires to take the next step in the relationship, saying, "I will search for the one my heart loves. So I looked for him but did not find him. The watchmen found me as they made their rounds in the city. 'Have you seen the one my heart loves?'" She has gone out into the night and walked through the city streets and square looking for the man she loves. While she is looking for him the watchmen find her and she asks them if they have seen him. We could wonder about all sorts of things here. Why couldn't she find him? Where was he? Remember that this is poetry and not a story, and the poet is not interested in developing the plot and details of a story. This poetry is a description of the woman's feelings and actions. Her frantic search in the night through the whole city reveals her devotion to the man she loves. The intensity of her emotion drives her out at night into the streets and squares of the city to hunt for him, a very dangerous thing for a woman to do. She does not give her actions a second thought, and that reveals the depth of her love for him.

Finding her beloved

In the fourth verse the woman is suddenly successful in her search: "Scarcely had I passed the watchmen when I found the one my heart loves" (3:4). Where she found him or where he had been are not important. The important thing is that after a frantic search she found the one her heart loves. Her search for him was difficult and dangerous even, suggesting that love is not just something that happens but it is something that couples need to put effort into. Some couples speak about finding love at first sight when they met, but many others say that when they first met their future husband or wife they did not feel any special attraction at all. Love is not something that most couples have instantaneously, but it can be something that requires effort and work. It seems to me that the woman's words in these verses are not so much about physically searching for and finding the man, but about pursuing and finding a heart connection with him. She is successful as she connects with him on a heart-to-heart level. As her love grows and deepens, she desires a lifelong commitment. The desire to leave your parents and be joined to the one you love is something that will grow as you build your relationship. Over time, you will begin to realize that you have found love and that you are ready to make this commitment.

This image of searching out love and the growing desire for commitment in this stage of their relationship should remind us again of the relationship we have with the Lord Jesus Christ. In Deuteronomy 4, Moses commands the people to put aside their idols and to serve the Lord God alone, saying in verse 29, "If you seek the LORD your God, you will find him if you look for him with all your heart and with all your soul." This language is similar to that used by the woman. God's promise is that if you look for him with all your heart, you will find him. The same thought is found in numerous other places in the bible. In Jeremiah 29:13 God says, "You will seek me and find me when you seek me with all your heart. I will be found by you." The apostle Paul tells the Athenians in Acts 17:27, "God did this so men would seek him and perhaps reach out for him and find him, though he is not far from each one of us." God is not a God who is far away, and therefore he commands us to make every effort to reach out and seek a relationship with him. And when we do, he gives this wonderful assurance that we will find him.

The Lord God clearly wants to enter into a love relationship with his people. We can see this through the love he has always shown them. In the Old Testament, God's love was clearly displayed in Egypt when he delivered his people out of slavery. In the New

Testament, his love is revealed in the life of his Son, Jesus Christ, who gave himself as the great sacrifice for us. God came near to us on this earth because he wants us to find him. When we have found him, our relationship with the Lord grows as we learn everything we can about him so that we begin to feel a heartfelt desire burning in our heart for him. As the woman in this song got to know the man, a desire for him grew within her. When you come to know Jesus Christ and to understand his great reputation as the Saviour of the world then you will also begin to long for him in your heart. When you truly understand the great sacrifice he has made for you on the cross because of his great love for you, then you will also experience that desire to seek him out in faith because your only hope rests in him. Then he has become your only joy.

God has made a wonderful promise that when we seek Jesus Christ as the one whom we love, we will find him. In the course of my ministry there have been many people who spoke about difficulties and struggles in their life, and how there were times when it seemed as if the Lord God was far away and they felt so lonely. At those times the burdens of life can seem unbearable and the joy of life disappears. In those dark moments, God's children long for their Saviour Jesus Christ, and from the darkness they cry out and search for the Lord God with their whole heart. Many can attest to the joy of finally being comforted when they reached out to the Lord in prayer. The Lord comes to support and strengthen us when we least expect it. Then you can indeed testify that you have found the one that your heart loves.

I came across an interesting connection between this text and the story of Mary Magdalene who also searched for one she loved on Easter Sunday (Lundbom 172–5). On that day, Mary Magdalene went to the tomb of Jesus, but it was empty (John 20:10–18). She saw two angels at the tomb (although at the time she did not know they were angels) and said to them, "They have taken away my Lord, and I do not know where they have laid him." These angels, just like the watchmen the woman meets in this song, do not give her an answer. After she spoke to the angels, Mary immediately turned around and saw the Lord Jesus standing there, but she did not recognize him because she was weeping and thought that it must be the gardener.

She asked him if he had taken away the body of Jesus. Then Jesus said, "Mary," and with joy she responded, "Rabboni!" There is an uncanny similarity between this story and the poem in Song of Songs 3:1–4. Remember how earlier in the gospel the Lord Jesus had cast seven demons out of Mary (Luke 8:2). She had lived until then in the grasp of the demons and the Lord Jesus had freed her from that prison. To her, this must have been like discovering a little of paradise on earth as she enjoyed freedom from the forces of darkness. No wonder then that she loved her Lord with all her heart and soul, and why she so intensely sought the body of the one whom she loved. By searching, she suddenly finds her Lord. But she does not just find his body, she finds the resurrected and living Lord. What joy to find the one on whom her whole life depended, the man on whom she had set her heart, and it is the reason that when she sees him she wants to fling her arms around him and hold him. We can understand why so many have theorized that there was a special relationship between Jesus and Mary. It would have been an intense and loving connection, but all these theories miss the point that the love Mary has for Jesus is love for him as her Saviour. She wants to hold on to him, to never let him go, because he is her only hope. She has found the one who has given her life.

Holding her beloved

The woman in the song expresses the same desire to hold on to her love, saying in 3:4, "I held him and would not let him go till I had brought him to my mother's house, to the room of the one who conceived me." She has found the man her heart loves, and she throws her arms around him, refusing to let him go, holding on and clinging to him until she has brought him "to the room of the one who conceived her." Why does she bring him to her mother's house? Bringing him there and taking him to her mother's room denotes that the relationship has become official. In Genesis 24:67, Isaac meets Rebekah and takes her to be his wife. That action is described with the words, "Isaac brought her into the tent of his mother Sarah, and he married Rebekah." In his mother's tent, the place where Isaac himself was likely conceived, Rebekah becomes his wife. This woman holds on to this man until she brings him to her mother's house as a sign that she will not let him go until they have made a commitment to marriage. She desires this man for her husband. That is where every love relationship should be heading. There is something wrong with a relationship if the couple does not feel a growing desire to leave their parents in order to become one. As love awakens, it will lead to this desire to hold on to the one you love in a committed marriage relationship.

And then as the text comes to this high point at which the woman declares her desire, we once again hear the warning not to arouse or awaken love "until it so desires." The woman warns the daughters of Jerusalem that desire for love is very powerful and it can be dangerous if it is not handled carefully. Do not awaken it until the time is right. This is a warning not to act impulsively, but instead to give careful consideration to what you are doing. Do not be in a hurry to commit to a relationship, but first be sure that the man or the woman is the right one for you. Most couples experience some doubts about different things during the courtship, but you should know each other well enough to know whether the man or the woman you desire stands on the same foundation as you. That foundation must be Jesus Christ. Is there a mutual desire to submit your life and your marriage to the will of your Saviour, Jesus Christ? That is crucial in your decision to move forward into a lifetime commitment to marriage.

The word the woman uses to express that she will not let go of the man she loves is the same word used by God in his promise to the people of Israel that he will never let them go. In Deuteronomy 31:6–8, the Lord promises that when Israel enters into the Promised Land he will go before his people to conquer the land for them. Then he says, "I will never leave you nor forsake you." When the Lord enters into a living relationship with us it means that he will never let us go. His promise is that he will always be faithful to us, because in his covenant he has entered into a committed relationship with us. God's people never need to doubt God's love. Although we often become unfaithful, God always remains faithful. You may always trust his promise to care for you.

God's care has been wonderfully revealed to us through Jesus Christ. It is the reason why Mary Magdalene did not want to let go of her Lord. She experienced his wonderful love when he freed her from the seven demons. Why would anyone want to let go of the one who has given them such a wonderful freedom and such a great sense of hope for the future? But there is also an important difference between this section of the song and the story of Mary Magdalene. Jesus says to her, "Do not hold on to me, because I have not yet ascended to the Father" (John 20:17). Mary Magdalene wants to hold on to him and claim him all for herself, but she is not allowed to because first Jesus needs to go to his Father's house in heaven. Mary cannot take him to her mother's house; instead, he will take her, together with all his disciples and believers, to the house of his Father. We have a great bridegroom who is preparing a place for us in his Father's house and the day is coming when the great bridegroom will appear from heaven and he will take his bride to himself in eternal glory. Is Jesus Christ the one for whom you long with your whole heart? He needs to be the love of your life.

For Further Reflection

1. Love creates such strong emotions that a person will seek to give their soul to the one they love. How can these powerful desires and emotions be used either for good or for destructive purposes in our search for a relationship?
2. Having found the one you love, how does your love for him or her grow? Is that principle also reflected in your love for Christ? Have you found Christ in faith and has that impacted your love and desire for him? Explain how the story of Mary Magdalene illustrates this principle in the life of God's people.
3. Why does the woman bring the man to her mother's home? Discuss how this reflects the progress in a love relationship.
4. A healthy relationship develops when there is a desire to leave father and mother and cling to the one you love in a committed marriage relationship. Is that happening in your relationship?
5. How does God describe his commitment to his people? How does this impact your commitment to your beloved?

Chapter 7

The Wedding Day Ordained by God

Who is this coming up from the wilderness
like a column of smoke,
perfumed with myrrh and incense
made from all the spices of the merchant?
Look! It is Solomon's carriage,
escorted by sixty warriors,
the noblest of Israel,
all of them wearing the sword,
all experienced in battle,
each with his sword at his side,
prepared for the terrors of the night.
King Solomon made for himself the carriage;
he made it of wood from Lebanon.
Its posts he made of silver,
its base of gold.
Its seat was upholstered with purple,
its interior inlaid with love.
Daughters of Jerusalem,
come out, and look, you daughters of Zion.
Look on King Solomon wearing a crown,
the crown with which his mother crowned him
on the day of his wedding,
the day his heart rejoiced.
(Song of Songs 3:6–11)

The bridegroom comes

*T*he refrain in 3:5, "Daughters of Jerusalem, I charge you by the gazelles and by the does of the field: Do not arouse or awaken love until it so desires," marks the end of the previous section. It also alerts us to a change in scene and that the relationship will now be explored from a different perspective. A new section begins in 3:6 with the words, "Who is this coming up from the desert like a column of smoke, perfumed with myrrh and incense made from all the spices of the merchant?" Although it is unclear who is speaking these words,[1] our attention is drawn to the fact that someone is coming up out of the wilderness. There is a column of smoke rising from there, perfumed with myrrh and incense and made from all the spices of the merchant. These are expensive spices and scents that merchants would purchase from exotic places in the world. Whoever is coming up from the wilderness must be a very important person, and the following verses confirm this, referring three times to King Solomon. Verse 7 tells us, "Look! It is Solomon's carriage." Again, in verse 9, we read, "King Solomon made for himself the carriage," and then the third instance, in verse 11, "Look at King Solomon wearing the crown." Solomon is coming up from the wilderness like a column of smoke in great splendor, and from verse 11 we conclude that he is coming to meet his bride on their wedding day. Many have concluded from this passage that the male character of this song must be Solomon. I argue instead that the couple in this song cannot be identified as any particular couple in Israel, but that every couple in Israel should be able to relate to the couple in this song.

So how does this reference to Solomon fit into the song?[2] In the first place, throughout the song there is usually some interaction between the man and woman. They are either describing the other's beauty or speaking about their love for each other. Up to this point, this song has tended to be very personal, but that is not the case in this passage. There is no description of Solomon himself, and neither do we hear anything about his love for the woman he is about to marry. Instead, this passage (3:6–11), gives only a description of Solomon's riches and possessions on his wedding day.

We can compare the lavishness of Solomon's wedding to that of the couple in this song. Some argue that the contrast which emerges answers the question of who has a better marriage relationship: is it Solomon with his many wives or the couple who faithfully love one another only? There is no indication in the text that the wedding description is meant to be used in this way. This passage describes the pomp and ceremony and splendour of Solomon's wedding day, and nothing is said at all about the quality of his relationship with his wives. When the poet describes Solomon's wedding day, that wedding is the standard against which every couple in Israel measures their own wedding. Remember that when Solomon got married, it was the first royal wedding of a prince who would become king in Israel.[3] In addition, Solomon's reign is also remembered as the most glorious reign in Israel because God not only made him very wise but also very rich. Therefore, Solomon's wedding must have been a glorious wedding. Every couple in Israel would dream of such a lavish wedding day. Three weeks before my wife and I were married, we watched the wedding of Prince Charles and Lady Diana Spencer. While their marriage ended tragically, at the time everyone was enthralled by the wedding and stood in awe at the splendour and beauty of it. It was a fairytale wedding that couples at the time could only dream of having. That wedding set the standard as one of the greatest weddings for that generation, while today it has been set by Prince William and Kate Middleton. And just like any couple today can dream about a wedding like William and Kate's, couples in Israel could only dream of a wedding like that of Solomon.

Verse 11 describes King Solomon as wearing the crown that his mother had crowned him with on his wedding day. We can only speculate about the procedure that was followed on that day as scripture does not give any details about Solomon's actual wedding ceremony. It is unlikely that the crown is the royal crown but a special wedding crown given to the bridegroom (Longman 139). We are not familiar with the customs in Solomon's time, but we do know that much later it was the custom in Israel for both the bride and groom to wear crowns at their wedding, and it is possible that the tradition dates back to when this song was written. Wedding crowns symbolized that the bridal couple were royalty in their own home. One might say that a man is king of his castle and the woman is queen of her home. It is fitting for every marriage to be regarded as a royal wedding. The description of the splendour at Solomon's wedding indicates to every couple in Israel the importance of their wedding day. This is a day that was ordained by God, so even the king went up to be married. If the king of Israel got married, then the people in the land are also expected to marry. Marriage was an important institution in Israel, and no couple in Israel could live together unless they were married.

The song reveals that the principle God laid down in the beginning with Adam and Eve continued to be an important one in Israel. At creation, the Lord made the woman, Eve, and gave her to the man, Adam. By doing this, God instituted marriage so that the man and woman became one (Genesis 2:24). In today's culture the principle of marriage is being undermined. Not so long ago, a British government minister was quoted as saying that a family with one husband and one wife was a lost cause.[4] Today, many people no longer believe that God ordains marriage, nor do they believe that when we reject God's ordained demands we bring calamity upon ourselves. Rather than an institution given by God, marriage is considered to be an old cultural tradition. Most still think that a wedding is a beautiful ceremony with some sentimental value but argue that it is not necessary for a real marriage.

While it is true that the pomp of the wedding ceremony is not important, the legal commitment that a couple makes to each other, as indicated by the marriage license, is important. The argument that the legal commitment of marriage is unnecessary can be compared to the argument that you do not need a driver's license to drive a car. It is true that you might be able to drive a car without a driver's license, but that does not mean you are free to drive a car. In the same way, you are not free to live together and to enjoy sexual intimacy until you have your marriage license. The wedding ceremony gives you the freedom to enjoy the marriage relationship. Of course, the importance of the marriage ceremony is not in receiving a legal document allowing you to live together, but it is in the wonderful vows you have made to each other before the Lord. You have made a life-long commitment to each other, and the certificate means that the government will hold you to the commitments you have made. The most beautiful aspect of the wedding is that in it a man and woman each promise to give themselves wholeheartedly to each other. They commit themselves to be each other's possession and promise to be faithful to one another for the rest of their lives.

The wedding day is one of the most joyful days in a person's life. Verse 11 says that for Solomon his wedding day was "the day his heart rejoiced." This song directly associates the joy of the heart with the commitment made to marriage—a couple finds real joy in their relationship when each makes a commitment to the other. It seals their love for each other for a lifetime. The joy in this song reflects the joy of the first marriage when Adam's heart overflowed with the greatest joy he ever experienced because God gave him Eve. Adam responded with a song, "This is now bone of my bones and flesh of my flesh; she shall be called 'woman,' for she was taken out of man" (Genesis 2:23).

The mention of Solomon here in the song brings the reader's attention to the Lord God, as Solomon was the theocratic king in Israel and, therefore, he represented the Lord. The image of Solomon as God's representative coming up from the desert like a column of smoke reminds us of the events at Israel's exodus from Egypt when the Lord came to his people in the pillar of cloud in order to lead them through the wilderness (Exodus 13:21–22). Mention of a column of smoke reminds the people of Israel that the Lord came to them in the wilderness and claimed them for his very own people, or as his bride. For the Lord God, as well as for the people of Israel, it was a joyous event that culminated with the Lord making a covenant commitment with Israel at Mount Sinai. God promised that he would be their God, and the people promised that they would be his people (Exodus 6:7). Then, in the New Testament, the Lord Jesus refers to Solomon, reminding the people that someone greater than Solomon had come to them, referring to himself as a bridegroom (Luke 11:31). Jesus Christ came to this world as the great bridegroom in order that through his sacrifice he might purify his bride from all her sins. There was great joy among the angels on Christmas day when they praised God before the shepherds, and the shepherds experienced great joy when they saw the Saviour lying in a manger in Bethlehem. They praised God for the birth of the Redeemer. Great joy came into the world when the bridegroom came to redeem his bride.

While believers in the Old Testament could already sing this song with great joy, remembering that the Lord God came up to them from the desert like a column of smoke, this song has even greater significance for us today as we know that Jesus Christ, who is greater than Solomon, is our great bridegroom. Since he committed his whole life to us, it is now our greatest joy to commit our whole life to him, and we now look for the great bridegroom to come for us from heaven. When he comes, his glory and splendour will be infinitely greater than Solomon's. Then he will take his bride to himself into eternal glory.

The bridegroom comes in splendour

What glory the bridegroom has! Solomon's splendour and glory is revealed in the descriptions of his carriage and his mighty warriors. The carriage itself was a litter, or palanquin, which is a chair or couch with a canopy and is carried on the shoulders of his warriors. The people thus see the king carried in a litter surrounded by sixty warriors, the noblest in Israel, to escort him. In 2 Samuel 23, David had thirty warriors to accompany him compared to his son Solomon's sixty, which seems to highlight that Solomon's splendour was greater than that of his father, David. King Solomon comes with strength as well, for every one of his warriors is experienced in battle, wearing weapons and fully prepared for any terror that might come in the night. What a picture for his bride to behold! She sees his strength and ability to protect her. This is a man with whom she can feel safe and secure.

In this, Solomon provides something that every bride must look for in her bridegroom. Earlier in this song the woman spoke about how safe and secure she felt in the care of the man whom she loves. He might not have the resources Solomon has, or sixty warriors to defend them, but then only the king and his family need that kind of security. A man must have the ability to provide a safe and secure environment for the woman he loves, and a woman needs to feel safe with the man she will marry. If that sense of security is not present during your courtship, you cannot hope that after you are married things will change and that then he will give you the protection you need. On your wedding day, the man that you are going to meet at the end of the aisle must be someone you can trust and with whom you can feel completely secure. As a man, the only way to understand and give your beloved the security she needs is to first make a personal commitment to Jesus Christ. To understand what it is to be a caring man is only possible if you first know the care that Jesus has for you. A godly woman is not looking for a man with a lot of brawn and physical strength but for someone that she can trust. This will be someone who is concerned about her well-being and ready to help her when she needs it. Knowing the love and care of Christ for you will allow you to begin to understand the love and care that your wife needs.

But adequate resources are important to a woman as well. The song (3:9–10) gives us a wonderful description of Solomon's carriage. It is made from the finest wood from Lebanon, with posts made of silver, a base of gold and upholstered in purple cloth, the colour of royalty. Its interior is lovingly inlaid by the daughters of Jerusalem.[5] This carriage is a display of Solomon's great wealth. When the bride sees him coming, she not only sees his great strength but also his great wealth; he is not only able to protect her, but he is also able to provide for her. The man in this song, unlike King Solomon, is a shepherd who takes care of the sheep, but he is willing to work hard and use the resources he has to support his wife. If there are no means for financially supporting the newly formed household, marriage becomes very difficult, if not impossible. No couple can live on love alone, and therefore they need to be reasonably certain that they have the means to support their household. From a man's perspective, his task is to be prepared and able to provide materially and financially for his wife and family. From a biblical perspective, it is primarily the husband's role to care for the material well-being of his family (Genesis 3:17–19), although it should be clear that the wife also has a task to make and take economic decisions for the well-being of the household (Proverbs 31:10–31). When a couple enters into a serious relationship, they first need to look at their own financial stewardship. If a man squanders his money and does not have a financial plan for the future, how can any woman feel confident that he will be able to provide for his family in the future? The same principle is true for any woman since she will be actively involved in managing the financial resources of the household.

An individual's sense of responsibility can also be seen in the way he prepares himself for a future career. This might involve a commitment to higher education or skills training. A Christian man is motivated to develop the talents that the Lord has given so he may use them to support not only his wife and family but also the work of God's kingdom. No one can offer marriage to a girl if he cannot show her that she will not be dragged into a life of debt and waste and constant worry for the future. What plans are you making today, even if you are not yet in a relationship, to support a family and kingdom work in the future? The priorities you set in this area reveal the priorities of your life. Besides being able to provide for your household, the way you handle your current financial responsibilities will clearly indicate whether you have developed a godly sense of self-sacrifice. Your willingness to self-sacrifice will become evident in the way you deal with God's directive to give your first fruits to him out of thankfulness.[6] When you are reluctant or forgetful in giving back to the Lord, or on the other hand if you give willingly, you give a clear indication of whether you are willing to sacrifice not only for God but also for others. How can the girl you love ever be sure that you will be willing to sacrifice for her well-being if you are not willing to sacrifice for the Lord now? Many put their own needs and desires first and refuse to sacrifice those desires for the good of the family. That is not showing the kind of leadership the Lord requires you to give your family.

We know from the life of Christ that true love is about denying ourselves and being ready to sacrifice everything for the well-being of those we love. The wedding day is a joyous and happy celebration—for Solomon it was "the day his heart rejoiced"—when the marriage begins with the proper commitment. Love is never a partial commitment, but it demands everything in your life. If you are not ready to give everything, you will not experience real joy in your marriage relationship. The same principle is very clear in our relationship with the Lord. The Lord Jesus revealed the depth of his love for us when he gave everything, even his very own life on the cross. He did not come to this world with great power, but with great humility. In fact, he was despised because he appeared to be so weak (Isaiah 53:3, Matthew 16:21, Luke 18:31–33). He was willing to be humiliated, willing to be abused by his people, willing to suffer persecution and, finally, willing to endure the agony of hell on the cross. Although Jesus appeared to be weak, in weakness he won the great victory. In addition to all that, he came without the glory and riches he had in heaven and his life on earth was one of great poverty and humiliation (Philippians 2:6–7). When the people saw him during his ministry on earth, they saw a poor teacher without material wealth. But by appearing in this way, Christ delivered his bride from the great tyranny of sin and evil. We can be totally secure in the knowledge that through his suffering and death he has saved us from all the forces of darkness. He is our great protector in whom we trust. And he has also made his bride incredibly rich, obtaining for us all the riches of the kingdom of heaven.

Because of this, the bride of Christ eagerly awaits her bridegroom from heaven. His return will be different from his first coming. The next time, he will come from heaven with his army of angels and the archangel sounding the trumpet to announce his coming. Then everyone will fall on their knees and acknowledge his great power. His coming will be in great splendour so that everyone will see his great glory. It will be a day of great fear and regret for all those who scoffed at him, but for the bride of Christ it will be a great day of joy. Therefore this song sung by the believers in the Old Testament takes on even greater meaning for the New Testament church. As the bride of Christ we have a bridegroom in whom we have eternal security. He will give to us the eternal riches of God's kingdom, and because of this we, the bride, praise and glorify our great bridegroom, Jesus Christ.

For Further Reflection

1. How might Solomon's lavish wedding impact young couples in Israel? Is it fitting that a marriage be compared to a royal wedding and if so, how?

2. Do you see marriage as an old tradition that is no longer relevant in our cultural situation, or do you believe that marriage is a God-ordained institution that is critical for the well-being of society? What role should God's Word play in this discussion?

3. In our culture many no longer see value in becoming married. What is the value of a marriage commitment for the long-term health of the relationship?

4. Why does marriage bring so much joy (Solomon speaks about "the day his heart rejoiced") to a couple?

5. Solomon's coming up from the wilderness in a column of smoke reminds the reader of God coming to his people in the wilderness in a column of smoke and entering into a covenant relationship with them. What joy does this give us today when we think of Christ who came as the great bridegroom?

6. What does the description of Solomon say about the qualities a man should strive to develop in order to be the husband his wife can feel secure with?

7. How does Christ's sacrifice speak about the sacrifices couples need to be willing to make in their marriage relationships?

Chapter 8

The Wedding Night

How beautiful you are, my darling!
Oh, how beautiful!
Your eyes behind your veil are doves.
Your hair is like a flock of goats
descending from the hills of Gilead.
Your teeth are like a flock of sheep just shorn,
coming up from the washing.
Each has its twin;
not one of them is alone.
Your lips are like a scarlet ribbon;
your mouth is lovely.
Your temples behind your veil are like the halves of a
pomegranate.
Your neck is like the tower of David,
built with courses of stone;
on it hang a thousand shields, all of them shields of warriors.
Your breasts are like two fawns,
like twin fawns of a gazelle that browse among the lilies.
Until the day breaks and the shadows flee,
I will go to the mountain of myrrh and to the hill of incense.
You are altogether beautiful, my darling;
there is no flaw in you.
Come with me from Lebanon, my bride,

come with me from Lebanon.
Descend from the crest of Amana, from the top of Senir,
the summit of Hermon,
from the lions' dens and the mountain haunts of leopards.
(Song of Songs 4:1–8)

*E*arlier on we noted that there is a natural progression in the communication of a young couple. At first they speak about what
is happening in their lives—school or their occupations, friends they
may have in common and the things they enjoy doing. But as time
moves on they want a deeper understanding of each other, and to
know the motivations that live in the other's heart. And as they learn
more about each other, they will also want to know each other in an
intimate, sexual way. As a healthy relationship develops, the desire to
"cleave to one another and become one flesh" (Genesis 2:24) grows.
This deepest intimacy cannot be shared, however, until the wedding
night when the couple receives God's blessing to celebrate their love
in the most intimate way. Therefore, having dealt with the description of the wedding in the previous chapter (3:6–11), the song now
moves on to describe the intimacy the couple now experiences on
their wedding night (4:1–5:1).

Sexuality: a gift of God

In the first part of this description, 4:1–7, the bridegroom outlines
the physical beauty of his bride using a common Arabic poetic device
called a *wasf*. In a *wasf* love poem, each part of a loved one's body is
described and praised in turn, using different metaphors. After he has
praised his bride for her beauty in this *wasf*, the groom invites her to
come to him so that they may consummate the marriage (4:8–5:1).
We will look at the man's description of his bride here and explore
the consummation itself in the next chapter.

Before I delve into the man's description of his wife with its
many sexual overtones, let me make a few observations. This passage
gives an explicit description of the sexual delight experienced by this
couple. There are a couple of dangers in attempting to interpret this
passage. One error is that we try to minimize the sexual language by

giving the text a spiritual meaning. This approach interprets the text allegorically and gives each image a spiritual meaning. The problem with this approach is that it loses sight of the wonderful sexual gift that the Lord has given in marriage. On the other hand, it is also a problem to focus on the sexual aspects of the text and regard marriage simply as a means of fulfilling our sexual desires, because then we lose proper respect for this wonderful gift.

Modern Western culture is obsessed with sexuality, and sex has become a commodity used to fulfill personal physical cravings. Today we hear about the "pornification" of society. Sexual images are everywhere, and pornography that in the past was limited to magazines sold at most corner stores has today become a huge industry accessible to anyone and everyone via the Internet. Movies often contain explicit sex scenes where the audience watches as a couple enjoys the most intimate part of a relationship. Behaviour considered inappropriate in the past has become mainstream today. All of this raises the question, how does this openness about sexuality affect marriage relationships? For many, the need for sex is a craving to be satisfied as if it is a hunger pang. The sad reality is that sex has become a very selfish pursuit having nothing to do with love or intimacy anymore, and its purpose is one's own gratification. It has become a commodity to be bought and used to fill our own needs. Christians are not immune to society's views on sexuality, and we are bombarded with it every day through the print media, advertising and the film industry. These images cause us to lose the proper perspective on our marriage relationship, and they will definitely warp the most intimate aspect of marriage if we don't protect ourselves from them.

As we examine the way the man in the song describes his wife, we need to keep in mind what the Lord reveals in Ephesians 5:31–32. Paul writes to the Ephesians that a man will leave his father and mother and be united with his wife, and the two will become one flesh. This oneness is not only a oneness in mind, heart and purpose—which no doubt need to be included otherwise the relationship is doomed—but when he speaks about "one flesh," Paul also has in mind the sexual union between husband and wife. He concludes with these words, "This is a profound mystery—but I am talking about Christ and the church." The great mystery that Paul refers to here is the love that a husband and wife experience when they become one flesh. When a husband and wife become one, not only in heart and mind but also in the conjugal act, they experience a love that is very deep, self-sacrificing and tender. They experience a love that to some degree reflects the intimate love of Christ for his church. The marvelous love of Christ is a love so tender and self-sacrificing that he was willing to suffer his whole life, even willing to endure the anguish of hell, for his bride. A husband and wife's greatest expression of their love is experienced in this most intimate act of marriage. That is why adultery is so devastating to a marriage relationship. The words of the bridegroom in this *wasf* need to be understood in the light of what Christ has done for his church. Looking at them in this way will prevent us from regarding the sexual act in marriage as something by which we can satisfy our own desires and instead allow us to see it as a means for us to express our deepest love and affection for our spouse.

Delight expressed in the bride

In the song, the bride and groom have entered into their marriage chamber, an intimate place where they can consummate their marriage. The bridegroom looks at his bride and speaks to her about his tender love and care for her. He tells her how beautiful she is and how everything about her completely satisfies him. She is perfect and wonderful in his eyes. Any man who truly loves his wife will take the time to speak to her about how lovely she is to him. A man who is only interested in fulfilling his own desires will not take the time for that; he will just take what he thinks rightfully belongs to him, with the result that his wife experiences sex as lust rather than love. In 4:1, this man says to his bride, "How beautiful you are, my darling! Oh, how beautiful!" He repeats those words in verse 7, creating a frame for the exclamations of admiration in verses 1–7. These expressions are set as poetry, where words are chosen to set a mood or convey certain ideas and feelings. It is a challenge to understand this poem today, some three thousand years later when the meanings of many of the expressions have been lost and it is difficult to relate to the language used.

He praises eight features of her body.[1] The bridegroom first describes the eyes of his beloved, saying, "Your eyes behind your veil are doves." It is likely that the bride wore a veil at her wedding, obscuring her face and adding a sense of mystery that heightens the man's excitement. Since he mentions cheeks in verse 3, it is likely that she is wearing a transparent veil over her entire face rather than one covering the lower half and exposing her eyes. Through the veil he sees her eyes and to him they are doves, or doves' eyes. While we have lost the sense of what having doves' eyes might mean, we do know that doves in the ancient Near East were closely associated with love and romance. Whatever the expression might mean, this man is very much attracted by her eyes. Her hair draws his attention as well: "Your hair is like a flock of goats descending from Mount Gilead." This conveys an image of black goats streaming down the slopes of Mount Gilead. The significance of a picture of Mount Gilead is lost to us also, but this mountain would have been visible off in the distance for many of the people of Israel, and they would see the flocks of black goats walking along the slopes, offering this beautiful image of wavy and flowing hair. He describes her teeth, "like a flock of sheep just shorn, coming up from the washing. Each has its twin; not one of them is alone." He finds her teeth beautiful—a fresh white colour like sheep just shorn and washed,[2] and each with its twin, meaning that the top and bottom teeth are matched and there are none missing. Without the benefits of cosmetic dentistry that we know today, the condition of the bride's teeth reflect that she is probably a young, healthy and well-cared-for individual.[3] It simply adds to the allure of her beauty. Her lips are like a scarlet ribbon and her mouth is lovely. He wants to kiss her lovely lips. Then his eyes move to her temples behind the veil, and these appear to him as if they are halves of pomegranates. The reference to her temples is unclear, and many think that he may actually be referring to her cheeks behind the veil. Perhaps he is reminded of the reddish-brown colour of the pomegranate and is complimenting her on her complexion. He describes her neck as like the tower of David that is "built with elegance." This is the only instance where the Hebrew word that is translated as "elegance" is used in scripture, making its meaning obscure.[4] We may have lost the sense of what the man really thinks about her neck, but it is certain is that he finds it very beautiful, like the tower of David. And on it hang a thousand shields, all of them shields of warriors. He may be thinking about the practice of soldiers hanging their decorated shields on the king's tower as he looks at a necklace she is wearing and notices how it enhances the beauty and elegance of her neck. In verse 5 he says about her breasts, "Your two breasts are like two fawns, like twin fawns of a gazelle that browse among the lilies." The gazelle is known for speed, sleekness and sensual beauty, and the reference to the fawn, or young gazelle, adds the image of pristine, youthful beauty. Whatever image the groom is conveying about her breasts, it is certainly one of sensual beauty.

What do we do with this description of the woman's body, and what is the message we need to take away from it? The problem with an allegorical approach is that the scriptures do not give any direction for assigning specific meanings to particular images, and the result is some absurd interpretations that cannot be justified from scripture. We should not focus on the minute details but instead keep in mind that these words convey a certain feeling and mood. The husband speaks about his love and fascination for his bride. He stands in awe of her beauty and thinks that he is the luckiest man on the earth to have her as his wife. In verse 6 he says, "Until the day breaks and the shadows flee, I will go to the mountain of myrrh and to the hill of incense." With these words he is responding to the woman's earlier invitation in 2:17, using many of her own words: "Until the day breaks and the shadows flee, turn, my lover, and be like a gazelle or like a young stag on the rugged hills." In chapter 2 she was looking forward to the wedding day and longing for the consummation of the marriage. Now it is their wedding night and the man responds: "I will go to the mountain of myrrh and to the hill of incense." He says, "The whole night I will take delight in you. All beautiful you are, my darling: there is no flaw in you." On his wedding night, this man now has the freedom to love his wife fully, as the Lord intended from the very beginning.

This passage makes it clear that love needs to be communicated not just with some actions but it also needs to be expressed with words. Love needs to be expressed by both husband and wife, but here it is the husband who has a lot to say to his wife about how he loves her. He takes the time to appreciate his bride and to convey to her how lovely and beautiful she is. She must have felt thrilled and reassured by the attention that her husband gives her, and it only serves to boast her self-confidence. He truly appreciates her, and in his love for her he only has eyes for his bride. He takes great delight in the wonderful gift that the Lord has given to him in her. The man's intimate description of his wife also reveals that love in a marriage relationship is physical and quite sensual. He speaks explicitly about how he takes delight in her physical attributes and that she satisfies him. His words are refreshing when you consider how every society sets its own standards for beauty; ours is no different, valuing unnatural slimness in a woman's body. As a result of cultural forces women are easily displeased with their proportions, and husbands who are critical of their wife's appearance can reinforce that negative self-image. We so easily allow the standards of society to become our measure for beauty. Husbands need to understand that allowing that to happen in your relationship destroys the intimacy in your marriage. This does not mean that you have to tell your spouse that she is the most beautiful person in the world. She will not believe you anyway, because she knows better than that. But true love says, "To me you are the most beautiful woman in the world, because you are very precious and dear to me. It is in you that I take delight and with you that I experience full satisfaction." As a husband you might easily take your wife for granted but you need to convey your ongoing appreciation to her. It may be as simple as expressing that to her from time to time, with words or a card or a small gift. In that way you build her up, and she will experience your heartfelt love.

We learn from this account of their wedding night that romance does not just happen on its own, but it takes ongoing attention and effort. A marriage relationship needs to be nurtured, and love needs your constant attention in order to grow. If you do not tend to the love in your relationship, it will die and leave you with a loveless marriage and there is no joy in such a marriage.

Turning again to the Ephesians reference, we can consider how the groom's words in these verses of the Song of Songs also reflect Christ's relationship to his church still today. The connection between the teaching concerning the Messiah (Saviour) and this song is very ancient, as it has been a Jewish tradition to read the Song of Songs during the Passover feast. The Jews connected this song to the Passover because they believed that the Passover "is a time of love between God and Israel" (Finch). The Passover celebration reminded the people of Israel of their time as slaves in Egypt when the Lord heard their cry for help and came to rescue them, renewing his covenant with them in which he promised that he would be their God and they would be his people. In this covenant, God was claiming Israel for himself and Israel became betrothed, or engaged, to the Lord God. The Israelites celebrated the first Passover on the night the Lord delivered them out of Egypt, but before they had left that country. At that Passover, God commanded the people to slaughter a lamb and to smear its blood on the doorposts of their houses. The blood of the lamb saved all the first-born children of Israel from death, because when the angel of the Lord saw the blood of the lamb on the doorpost of a house he passed over it, sparing the child. The lamb that was slaughtered on the Passover became the symbol for the great Lamb who would come and deliver his people from their sins (Isaiah 53:7; John 1:29).

In the Passover, the Lord revealed his great love for Israel. But why did God love them? Were they better or more deserving than other people? Not at all! They certainly were not the most attractive people in the world (see Ezekiel 16:1–7). Although they were unworthy, the Lord still spoke tenderly to the Israelites about his great love for them. He told them that they were the apple of his eye and that he took great delight in them (Deuteronomy 32:10). How could God say that? Did the Lord really mean that from his heart? Yes, he meant it with his whole heart. He spoke to them about his great love as if they were perfect, because they had been made perfect through the blood of the Lamb. Even though the great Lamb had not been slaughtered yet, the Passover lamb was a shadow of what was to come many centuries later. Today, we look back to the Lord Jesus as the great Passover Lamb who was slaughtered on the cross for us. He bought his bride, which is his church, with his precious blood and he takes great delight in her. He speaks to her about his great love, and because of that love for us we are able to respond in faith and give our life in faithful service to our bridegroom, Jesus Christ. It is that love of Christ that makes it possible for husbands to love their wives and for wives to respond to the love of their husbands with the greatest intimacy.

Protection offered to the bride

The man in our song continues to patiently and lovingly encourage his wife to yield herself to him completely in verse 8. He encourages her, saying, "Come with me from Lebanon, my bride, descend from the crest of Amana, from the top of Senir, the summit of Hermon, from the lions' dens and the mountain haunts of the leopards." She is not literally in Lebanon or on the crest of Amana or the top of Senir or the summit of Hermon, but these images describe her as being in a distant place, remote from him, and from which he encourages her to "come down" to him. But what is the role of the lions and leopards in this song? There are two possible scenarios: either the women is being protected by the lions and leopards there in the mountains, and the man is calling her to come out from the safety afforded by these animals and saying that he will protect her instead, or the lions and leopards are a danger to the woman and he is encouraging her to come out to the safety he will provide. In either case, he wants her to give up her fears and instinct of self-protection, and to trust him completely for her well-being. In the context of this song, it is their wedding day, the time for consummating the marriage, and the groom is encouraging his bride to yield herself to him completely. He wants her to leave her old life and to enter into a new secure relationship with him where he will always protect her in his love. In that context, it is understandable that the woman may be dealing with some fears and uncertainties on her wedding night. In his tender love for her he encourages her to come with him, telling her that she does not need to be afraid because he will take care of her. She can yield herself to him, fully secure in the knowledge that he will love her.

We are given a picture of a man that this woman can trust. He will protect her rather than abuse her or use her for his own purpose. The reality of sin means that men so often misuse their role and their physical strength in a relationship. Rather than maintaining a loving environment in which a wife is cherished and can grow, husbands can often be controlling and abusive. By behaving in this way, men do not establish an atmosphere where real love and romance can blossom, and in this unhealthy environment God's whole purpose for marriage is destroyed. In the Song of Songs, the Lord reveals his desire for our marriage relationship. This man says to his bride, "Come with me and I will protect you from the lions and leopards. In my love you will find security and joy, for it is my desire to love you with my whole heart."

When we reflect on this man's words, it reminds us of the way Jesus Christ speaks about us as his church and his bride. He assures us that we may surrender our whole life to his loving care. He assures us that he will protect us from the lions and leopards in this world. He is the good shepherd who defends the sheep against the lions and leopards that seek their destruction; he is willing to lay down his life for the sheep (John 10:11). Christ's love for us was so great that he gave his life on the cross so that we can enjoy life. Christ is not interested in using us to fulfill his own desires, but his only concern is that he might eternally secure our life with his blood.

When husbands live secure in this love of Christ, they can truly love their wives as God intended them to. In Christ's love it is possible to lay aside our own selfish desires in order to love our wives with our whole heart. It is through Christ's love that you can truly love your wife by protecting her and providing an atmosphere in which her love can blossom. And when you reflect that love of Christ in your relationship with your wife, she will enjoy a feeling of security, knowing that she is fully loved. In that wonderful marriage bond you can again reflect the love of your great bridegroom, Jesus Christ.

For Further Reflection

1. Different approaches have been used to deal with the sexually charged language of the song. Discuss some of those approaches and suggest a healthy way to approach this language in the song.

2. What effects do you think the obsession of modern culture with sexuality has on your own life and on your marriage relationship in particular? Discuss how you might guard yourself against those influences.

3. How does our relationship with Christ, as expressed by Paul in Ephesians 1, help us to properly deal with the *wasf* in which the man describes his wife?

4. What do the words of this *wasf* teach a husband about treating his wife? How do you speak to your wife and how do you show her that she is special to you? Discuss with your beloved how she thinks you see her and consider any changes you may need to make to encourage her.

5. Why was the Song of Songs read on Passover? How did the Passover reflect the love of God for his people?

6. How does Christ speak to his bride, his people? How do his words of love and care impact your life?

7. In connection with the consummation of the marriage, how does the husband provide an environment where his wife feels loved and not used? How does Christ provide a safe environment for his bride, the church?

Chapter 9

The Consummation

You have stolen my heart, my sister, my bride;
you have stolen my heart
with one glance of your eyes,
with one jewel of your necklace.
How delightful is your love, my sister, my bride!
How much more pleasing is your love than wine,
and the fragrance of your perfume, more than any spice!
Your lips drop sweetness as the honeycomb, my bride;
milk and honey are under your tongue.
The fragrance of your garments
is like the fragrance of Lebanon.
You are a garden locked up, my sister, my bride;
you are a spring enclosed, a sealed fountain.
Your plants are an orchard of pomegranates with choice fruits,
with henna and nard, nard and saffron, calamus and cinnamon,
with every kind of incense tree, with myrrh and aloes and all the
finest spices.
You are a garden fountain, a well of flowing water streaming down
from Lebanon.

Awake, north wind, and come, south wind!
Blow on my garden, that its fragrance may spread everywhere.
Let my beloved come into his garden and taste its choice fruits.

I have come into my garden, my sister, my bride;
I have gathered my myrrh with my spice.
I have eaten my honeycomb and my honey;
I have drunk my wine and my milk.
Eat, friends, and drink;
drink your fill of love.
(Song of Songs 4:9–5:1)

*A*fter the man has described and praised each part of his bride's body with a *wasf* love poem, the song now takes up the topic of the consummation of their marriage. This section of the song speaks about the most intimate aspect of marriage in a beautiful and wholesome way. The sexual relationship between a husband and wife is a beautiful gift from the Lord in which a man and woman may express their love for one another. It is God's intention that through this gift a husband and wife may grow in love and commitment.

The bride and the locked garden

As is often the case throughout this song, in this section the meaning of some of the images the groom uses to express his love and admiration of his bride are difficult for us to appreciate, but there can be no doubt that the words express overwhelming emotions as he sees his bride. Basically, he says, "My love for you is so great that you drive me crazy. With one glance of your eyes you set my heart racing, my sister, my bride." To describe your bride as your sister, as he does in verses 9 and 10, might be difficult for us to appreciate today in our culture, but for him the words clearly express love. In the ancient Near East the words "brother" or "sister" were used as terms of endearment by an intimate couple.[1] It likely conveys both the closeness of a brother-sister relationship as well as the commitment of marriage in which they become one flesh.

These verses not only speak about how beautiful she is in his eyes, but he also speaks about how her love for him delights him and is more pleasing than wine. Even her perfume intoxicates him! The fragrance of her perfume is more pleasing than any spice. Spice was an important luxury: for example, Queen Sheba gave it as a gift to

King Solomon when she visited him, and Esther used it to prepare herself to meet the king of Persia (1 Kings 10:10; Esther 2:12). The perfume that the woman of this song wears is more delightful to the groom than the most expensive spice used by the richest people in the world. Very subtly, but also very powerfully, he proclaims his great love for his bride.

His next words describe her lips: "Your lips drop sweetness as the honeycomb, my bride; milk and honey are under your tongue." Honey is a natural sweetener, and in the same way one enjoys honey he is attracted by what he describes as the wonderful sweetness of her lips, and he discovers milk and honey under her tongue. The expression "milk and honey" is often used to describe the richness and luxury of the Promised Land of Canaan. Her mouth is so luscious that he wants to keep tasting its sweetness. Proverbs 5:3–6 uses similar imagery that stands in contrast to the words of this text. There it says, "The lips of the adulteress drip with honey, and her speech is smoother than oil." This imagery describes the lips of an adulterous woman enticing men who desire to enjoy their sweetness. But once there, a man finds instead a taste as bitter as gall. The lips of the adulteress, although enticing, are deceitful, while the lips of the bride and her love are genuine. The lesson of this contrast is that we need to look for genuine love rather than an encounter based on lust and the need to fulfill sexual desire, which will always disappoint and be bitter as gall in the end. The genuine love depicted in this song, and which is pursued by this couple, is ultimately based on the love of Christ that will never disappoint. However, the reality in our lives is that there will always be disappointing moments in our relationship, but when our love is genuine we will learn to work through those disappointing moments and again find joy and happiness in our marriage. Then the sweetness of the lips of our beloved will always remain sweet to our taste.

This bride awakens all the senses of her bridegroom. He does not only delight in the sweetness of her lips but he also delights in the wonderful fragrance of her garments that smell like the pleasing aroma of the cedars of Lebanon. But his greatest delight is described in verse 12 where he says about his bride, "You are a garden locked up, my sister, my bride; you are a spring enclosed, a sealed fountain."

This image of a locked garden is an important theme that is picked up in later literary works. The image of the virgin as a locked garden is connected in medieval English literature to the tradition of courtly love in which the lover needed to go through certain trials in order to win the chaste love of his lady (Jeffrey 363). This later literary tradition properly understood the imagery of this song; the bride is a locked garden that no one could enter, because she has kept herself chaste for the one to whom she will give her love.

The image of the locked garden would have been well understood in the ancient Near East, because most homes had an inner courtyard in which some herbs as well as a grape vine or fig tree were planted (Keel 169). It would be an intimate place, tucked away from the eyes of the world. In the garden described in these verses there is also a locked spring and a sealed fountain. He says about his bride that she is "a garden fountain, a well of flowing water streaming down from Lebanon." He does not envision her as a cistern in which the rainwater is collected and after a period of time becomes stale and putrid. Instead, she is like flowing water that constantly refreshes the well with clear, fresh water. In fact, the water comes streaming down from Lebanon with its high, snow-capped mountains that feed the crystal-clear streams that run down the mountains all year round. This is the kind of water that is sweet and refreshing and such a pleasure to drink.

He also discovers choice fruits in this garden, with henna and nard and saffron, with calamus and cinnamon, with every kind of incense tree and with myrrh and aloes and all the finest spices. He finds a rich variety of trees and plants in the garden as well. The garden also contains an orchard of pomegranates, which are often associated with love. The word "orchard" is itself significant as the Septuagint translates the Hebrew word as "paradise,"[2] thereby presenting an allusion to the paradise of Genesis 2, which also had a river running through it to water the trees and plants of every kind. The Garden of Eden was the most beautiful place on the whole earth, where Adam and Eve could enjoy a great variety of riches in God's creation. In this reference, the groom describes his bride as a locked garden that contains everything a man could ever desire. She is like paradise to him, the place where he wants to be and where he can find everything he needs for his complete satisfaction and well-being.

As mentioned, he refers to her as a "locked garden," which we can understand to mean that her garden (paradise) is preserved for this man. She has kept it locked up so that no one else has been able to enjoy the pomegranates and choice fruits or the henna, nard and saffron, and no one else has been able to drink from her fountain. The point he makes is that she has kept herself sexually pure. The reference to her as a well echoes or reflects the words of Proverbs 5:15 where wisdom compares a man's wife to a well or cistern. There he warns the men of Israel to drink from their own cistern and not go after other women or prostitutes. Every man must look to his wife as the well or source of his refreshment, rejoicing in the wife of his youth and constantly being captivated by her love. This man takes great delight in the fact that his bride has locked her garden and kept her well for him alone. He may eat and drink from her and take great delight in the awareness that she has reserved herself for him. The message here is that men and women are to keep themselves sexually pure for the special person they will marry. Sadly, that is no longer the message that we hear in our society.

Here I need to interject that while the text speaks about the man taking great delight in his wife who has kept herself sexually pure as a locked garden for her husband, it should be clearly understood that scripture makes the same demand on men to keep their bodies pure for the woman they will marry. In some cultures men expect their wives to be virgins but the same demand is not always made on the men. The Lord places the same demand on both men and women to keep their bodies pure for marriage (see Proverbs 5:1– 20; 9:13–18). While writing this chapter, I came across an article about the latest sex education program in a major Western nation. The pamphlet under discussion encouraged youth in high school to enjoy sex and stated, "Enjoying sex is a natural and recommendable thing. Learn the best ways to enjoy it with security and tranquility." While God clearly indicates that we should keep our bodies pure, in most Western societies today it is "understood" that young people will experiment with their bodies and they are encouraged to do so freely but "safely." But God warns against this for a good reason:

failing to keep the garden of your body pure will have consequences for your marriage relationship.

Our choices and behaviours have consequences. You may try to hide or forget about things that you have done in the past, but past events will always be there and stand in the way of the relationship even if the person you love is not aware of it. There will always be some impact from the event, even if it is only that you can never erase the memory of it. When you marry, your greatest pleasure is to be able to unlock your garden and to open your well for the person that you love without any dark shadow hanging over the relationship. But what if there is such a shadow in your life, either through things that have happened to you or because of your own choices? We understand the nature of sin, and we also know that young people do fall into temptations that later on they regret with great sorrow. If this is the case, will you ever be able to experience the love that the couple in this song shares? While there will always be scars and regret, when there is real repentance it is possible to enjoy a wonderful intimacy in a marriage relationship. But for that to happen we have to consider our own relationship with Jesus Christ.

When Christ came to reveal his love for us, we were not locked gardens for Christ. The gardens of our lives were in disarray because of sin—we had no lock on the door and had let every manner of sin and corruption into our lives. In the Old Testament we find many examples of God speaking about the unfaithfulness of his people. Each time God reminded them of how they gave his gifts of grain and produce and wine to their lovers. They committed spiritual adultery each time they pursued relationships with foreign gods. When we understand the corruption of our hearts and the rebelliousness of our flesh against God, then we know that when Christ entered into a relationship with us we were defiled and corrupt and not able to offer him a heart that was a locked garden. Still, Christ came in mercy and spoke tenderly to us through his gospel. He promised to remove the effect of our sins and corruption. In his tender love, he commanded us to rebuild the wall around the garden of our life, to lock the gate and to replant the garden. It is the Lord Jesus who makes it possible for us to renew our life so that wickedness and sin no longer work freely in us. Through his redeeming work, Christ makes it possible to again tend the garden of our heart so that it produces fruits and flowers and spices for him.

Our bridegroom, Christ, takes great delight, as does the song's bridegroom with his bride, when he comes into our renewed gardens to feast on our fruits of thankfulness. Christ makes it possible for us to renew the dilapidated garden of our life, and he will also make it possible for you to rebuild your garden for the man or woman you love if you have ruined it in the past. If your garden has been spoiled because you did not lock it, you need to build a wall around your life and lock the gate. That is possible when you repent from sin. Then you can set your garden in order again and start to tend the fruit trees and the flowers and spices so that your garden will be a delight to someone with whom you share genuine love. While there is sadness about the past, there is also the joy that in Jesus Christ you can enjoy a new life.

The invitation into her garden

Now that the bridegroom has expressed his great delight in his bride and encouraged her to yield to his love, the bride unlocks her garden for her beloved, saying, "Awake, north wind, and come, south wind! Blow on my garden that its fragrance may spread abroad. Let my beloved come into his garden and taste its choice fruits." The woman uses the refrain "awake" a number of times in this song. Earlier, she warned the daughters of Jerusalem, "Do not arouse or awaken love until it so desires." Now the time has come to set aside this warning and let her desire for her beloved be fully awakened in her. She may now give in to her desire for the one she loves. She calls out to the wind from the north and the south to blow on her garden so that the fragrance of her spices will be spread around for her beloved to enjoy. She entices him and invites him to come into her garden to taste its choice fruits.

There is a subtle change in the way the woman uses the personal pronoun in verse 16. At first she commands the wind to blow on "my" garden, and then she invites her beloved come into "his" garden. Now that they are married she no longer thinks of her garden as just hers, because it now also belongs to him. Her body has become his so that they become one flesh in words that mirror Paul's when he says in 1 Corinthians 7:4, "The wife's body does not belong to her alone but also to her husband. In the same way, the husband's body does not belong to him alone but also to his wife." In this description, the woman freely gives herself, body and soul, to her husband. She is his possession and he is her possession.

When she invites her beloved to enter into her garden, she indicates that her greatest delight is to yield herself on their wedding night to the man who loves her so dearly and tenderly. She is delighted by the fact that she is able to satisfy him with the fruits of her garden. This is the delight of genuine love and respect for each other that a married couple has. This man does not just take what he might think is his right, but he speaks tenderly to her about his love, and she responds to his love by inviting him to enjoy her garden. Love never allows us to act as if it is our right to take what we want from each other. When a husband and wife enjoy a proper marriage relationship they will not take advantage of each other, because genuine love is about giving, not about taking. Love does not try to fulfill its own desires but it always cares for the one who is loved. That is the only principle on which any marriage relationship can flourish and grow.

As Paul's words indicate in the text mentioned above, the profound mystery of this oneness between husband and wife echoes the unity that the church (as the bride) has with Christ. Christ does not enter into a relationship with us in order to use us to fulfill his own desires. Having bought his bride with his blood, he speaks tenderly to her about his great love for her. It is a love so great that he was willing to sacrifice his life for her. Christ speaking to you about his tender love and mercy must create in your heart a deep desire to love him as your Lord and Saviour. When you know the love of Christ, then your greatest joy is to give your life to him as your bridegroom. Then you want to yield every part of your life to him, because your life is like a garden that has been restored by him.

In 5:1 the bridegroom responds, "I have come into my garden, my sister, my bride: I have gathered my myrrh and my spice. I have eaten my honeycomb and my honey; I have drunk my wine and my milk." The words indicate that the marriage has been consummated. Notice that he says, "I have come into my garden." This woman has given him a wonderful gift, and she is now his and he may eat from her garden and find refreshment at her well for the rest of their life. He has waited a long time to enter her garden and now that he has been given entry, he is fully satisfied. She has responded to his love with her love, and that is the way it should be in your marriage relationship. If instead you are only interested in satisfying your own sexual needs, taking but not giving, you will never be satisfied. That is lust rather than love, and scripture makes clear that lust never has enough; it always says "more, more" and is never satisfied (Proverbs 30:15–16; Ephesians 4:19). But if you truly love your spouse from the heart, you will experience a wonderful intimacy and the result is that you will be satisfied, because you will take pleasure in your mutual love for one another. This love is possible because of Christ's love for you.

Some readers might be skeptical about the possibility of experiencing a love like that in a marriage. Is this song too idealistic about what is possible in marriage? My wife suggested that after hearing me preach on this song, listeners might think that we have a perfect marriage. Unfortunately, every marriage has struggles and no couple is always able to sing the song that this couple sings. Selfishness and bitterness and envy and anger often enter our hearts, and these things negatively impact our marriage relationship so that we do not always experience the intimacy that we read about in this song. Sometimes, it is things from our past that stand in the way of intimacy. When a woman or a man has been sexually abused as a child it can impact how they experience the marriage relationship. Preoccupation with work or sports or friends can also get in the way of intimacy. We might wonder, since there are so many things that can negatively impact our marriage relationship, why does the Lord give us a song like this one? The love that this couple experiences might be discouraging rather than encouraging, since we do not always experience love this way. We need to remember that in the song the Lord reveals that although we live in a world that is broken by sin he has restored the possibility for a man and woman to again experience the marriage relationship in the way he intended it. When sin entered the world in the beginning, the possibility for marriage as we see it in the song disappeared, because our heart became corrupt with sinful desires and emotions. But through Christ, it is possible to change this.

The love Christ displayed for us on the cross made it possible for us to love again. In our marriages we are challenged daily to love each other as Christ loved us, but we do not need to get discouraged. In Christ we can move forward, for in faith we look to him to give us the strength to love our spouse again. And as you learn to love as Christ loves you, you will begin to experience a wonderful growth in your relationship. There will be ups and downs, times when you feel close and intimate and times when you do not feel it so much. But this song gives us the courage to go on, for it shows what love in a marriage can really be like. In the power of Christ we strive for that goal. God makes love possible again in a world that is full of selfishness and unfaithfulness. This song speaks wonderfully about that love.

The consummation under God's blessing

The last words at the end of the wedding night are, "Eat, friends, and drink; drink your fill of love." These words may have been spoken by the daughters of Jerusalem or they may have been inserted as an editorial comment. Although we cannot be certain about the speaker, the words clearly convey approval over the love this couple enjoys. And this approval is God's benediction on their marriage. The Lord gives his blessing on the consummation of their love.

In the history of the church, there have been periods where the reality of the sexual relationship in marriage was tolerated as a necessary evil only for the purpose of having children but not something to be discussed. The church has not always spoken in a positive or helpful way about sex in marriage. The result is that many believers have been confused about whether sexuality is something we may enjoy or something about which we need to be embarrassed and ashamed. Many people have felt guilty about enjoying sexual intimacy in their marriage. But in this song the Lord clearly encourages the couple to enjoy the most intimate part of marriage. He says, "Drink your fill of love." This couple has the Lord's blessing and may enjoy the sexual aspect of marriage without any guilt or shame. Keep in mind that God gives his blessing because this couple is enjoying this intimacy as a gift from him. There is no such blessing on this gift if it is not used in love. In a loveless relationship, sex only becomes a means for selfish gratification and a god to which you look to fill the lust of your heart. But when you are faithful to your spouse and use God's gift to express your deepest love and tender care for your spouse, then you will be richly blessed. Then you will experience a true oneness in the flesh, a unity that finds its greatest expression in the relationship you have with Christ Jesus as your Lord.

For Further Reflection

1. The bridegroom speaks about the sweet and enticing lips of his bride. How does the contrasting image of the enticing lips of the adulterous woman serve as a warning?

2. The image of the bride as a locked garden became an important literary theme in English literature. Does this theme still function in our culture today? How should this theme function in the life of God's people?

3. The poet makes a subtle connection between the woman as a locked garden and paradise. What does that reveal about the relationship every husband should have with his wife?

4. How does the unlocked garden reflect our spiritual condition when Christ came to us with the gospel? How does one repair a garden that has not been locked?

5. What, if any, significance is there in the fact that the woman invites her husband to come into "his" garden? What does Paul teach in 1 Corinthians 7:4 about the relationship between husband and wife?

6. How does genuine love reveal itself in the relationship between husband and wife? How does Christ reveal that genuine love in his relationship with his bride, the church?

7. What are some things that undermine intimacy in marriage? Are there things in your marriage that threaten your intimacy and what changes can you make to protect or restore that intimacy?

8. Discuss how sexuality has often been dealt with in the church and how that contrasts with the way this song speaks about it. What does this teach about how this issue should be approached?

Chapter 10

Marriage Troubles

I slept but my heart was awake.
Listen! My beloved is knocking:
"Open to me, my sister, my darling,
my dove, my flawless one.
My head is drenched with dew,
my hair with the dampness of the night."
I have taken off my robe—must I put it on again?
I have washed my feet—must I soil them again?
My beloved thrust his hand through the latch-opening;
my heart began to pound for him.
I arose to open for my beloved,
and my hands dripped with myrrh, my fingers with flowing myrrh,
on the handles of the bolt.
I opened for my beloved,
but my beloved had left; he was gone.
My heart sank at his departure.
I looked for him but did not find him.
I called him but he did not answer.
The watchmen found me as they made their rounds in the city.
They beat me, they bruised me; they took away my cloak,
those watchmen of the walls!
Daughters of Jerusalem, I charge you—
if you find my beloved, what will you tell him?

Tell him I am faint with love.
How is your beloved better than others,
most beautiful of women?
How is your beloved better than others,
that you so charge us?
My beloved is radiant and ruddy, outstanding among ten thousand.
His head is purest gold; his hair is wavy and black as a raven.
His eyes are like doves by the water streams, washed in milk,
mounted like jewels.
His cheeks are like beds of spice yielding perfume.
His lips are like lilies dripping with myrrh.
His arms are rods of gold set with topaz.
His body is like polished ivory decorated with lapis lazuli.
His legs are pillars of marble set on bases of pure gold.
His appearance is like Lebanon, choice as its cedars.
His mouth is sweetness itself; he is altogether lovely.
This is my beloved, this is my friend, daughters of Jerusalem.
(Song of Songs 5:2–16)

*I*n chapter 4 of the song, the bridal couple speaks of their wonderful experience on their wedding night and how they are completely smitten with one another. The reality, however, is that wedding night expectations do not always match the reality and couples are often disappointed. The wedding is usually a long and exhausting day of celebration, and when the couple is finally alone there is awkwardness as they experience a new phase in their relationship. But while the expectations may not be met, there is still the wonder of being able to experience this new phase together as they now enjoy sexual intimacy.

The time period after the wedding is a honeymoon stage during which a husband and wife enjoy the thrill of being together. They are attentive to each other's needs and their lives revolve around each other. But it is impossible to keep up the intensity experienced during this period, and this phase invariably comes to an end. Conflicts and difficulties begin to arise. A husband and wife begin to see each other more realistically. We see each other's faults and weaknesses, and those begin to bother us. As time passes, we begin to take the love for each other for granted. The Song of Songs recognizes this reality and does not end with the love poem about the wedding night, but it also deals with the struggles of marriage. Every marriage will have conflict and troubles; the question is not whether we will have conflict, but what are we going to do about the conflict. Love does not need to die off in the conflicts that come after the initial thrill of married life, and it can continue to grow and blossom. Conflicts in marriage should be understood as opportunities for love to grow and deepen.

The song's fifth chapter describes an instance of conflict in a marriage, a scenario in which the bride takes the love of her husband for granted. In this case, the husband responds by dealing with his wife wisely and lovingly. His reaction makes it possible for the bond of love to grow in the face of difficult challenges. The husband is portrayed as the perfect head of his wife because in his leadership role he shows love and great respect for her. He does not react to her selfish actions in a personally aggrieved or self-centred way, but he works in the best interest of the relationship. The result of his wisdom and strength of character is that the bond of love in this marriage flourishes.

The bride's selfish response

The events of 5:2–6:3, as told from the perspective of the bride, are surreal—that is, rather than describing an actual event, the words set a tone or establish a mood for an imagined scenario. The incident, "I slept but my heart was awake. Listen! My lover is knocking," along with other interactions described throughout this section, use images that do not make sense in real life.

The woman hears her beloved calling out to her, "Open to me my sister, my darling, my dove, my flawless one. My head is drenched with dew, my hair with the dampness of the night." In this scenario the woman has already gone to bed and he does not have a key to the room. Rather than raise questions about the realism of this situation and become bogged down in the details of the story, we should simply keep in the mind that the poet is setting a mood and not lose sight of the multiple layers of meaning here (Longman 166). The man's request for admission to her room conveys a request for sexual intimacy. He tells her that his head is drenched with dew from the dampness of the night, signifying that he wants her to know that he has gone through some uncomfortable conditions to be with her. He was out in the night, perhaps busy taking care of some chore that needed to be done in the field. Now he is happy to be home and looking forward to an intimate moment with his wife. He "knocks at her door," asking her to open it for him. He expresses his love for her, calling her "my sister, my darling, my dove, my flawless one," endearments we have seen earlier in this song. In that time era, as they do in this context, these terms express his great love and respect for his bride in a clear and forceful way. With these words his love for her cannot be mistaken.

But she does not respond in a positive way, instead saying, "I have taken off my robe—must I put it on again? I have washed my feet—must I soil them again?" Her words, expressing a reluctance to get her feet dirty or to get dressed again, actually say, "I don't really want to deal with you right now." This is a very different behaviour than the one she showed earlier in their relationship. In the third chapter of the song, she was lying on her bed worrying about losing the man she loved. At that time she got up in the middle of the night to find him and to take him home to her parents to make the engagement official. At that time her love for him was so overwhelming she could not stop herself from going out and searching for him all over the city. Now she is married and he has committed himself to her, it seems as if she takes his love for granted.

These verses reflect a reality that is often present in our marriages. Husbands and wives can become so busy with the routines of earning a living, running a household and raising children that they don't have the time or energy to devote proper attention to each other. Today our lives are a constant round of stresses and problems that demand our attention, and at the end of the day we cannot find the energy or the desire to be interested in or involved in each other's lives, and we no longer nurture our love for each other. Husband and wife easily begin to take each other for granted, and the love that was experienced during courtship and the early days of marriage begins to fade. At the beginning we were eager to look after the needs of the one we love, but in marriage those requests can easily feel like burdens. Instead of having a desire to help and assist each other, we are easily irritated and resentful so that we refuse to serve one another out of love.

This common situation in marriage is also common in our relationships with Jesus Christ. We are distracted in our service to Christ by the same things that distract us in our marriage relationship. I am so grateful when I see God's youth display a passionate desire to serve the Lord. But I also notice that when these young adults begin to pursue a career or other interests this enthusiasm can waver. As they mature and marry, they take on the responsibility of children and family, they begin to feel the pressures of life and their youthful zeal to serve the Lord can begin to wane. This marks the beginning of taking what we have with the Lord Jesus for granted so that when he comes knocking at our door we are too busy to answer him. When our love for the Lord Jesus is not a priority and we let ourselves be distracted by daily pressures our commitment to serve him with our whole life wavers. We continue to expect Jesus Christ to serve us and to fulfill all our needs, but our responsibilities in serving the Lord Jesus can irritate us and make us resentful. Our attitude to Christ can change so quickly that we become ungrateful for and uncaring about his great love for us. As the bride of Christ, our attention and devotion must be centred on our bridegroom so that when he comes knocking at the door of our heart, we will jump to open the door and embrace him as the one who is dear to our heart.

Our fervent love for Jesus Christ must be reflected in our marriage. If there is anything that turns your heart away from your spouse or is a distraction to your relationship, then you can relate to this woman's struggle. On a certain level she loves her husband, but finding her robe and dirtying her feet when it is inconvenient for her are not things she is prepared to do for him. She has allowed herself to be less than diligent in her relationship, something that is often the root of struggles in marriage relationships. Regaining the passion in marriage is done first of all by recognizing again the tremendous gift the Lord has given us in our spouse. Think back to the day when you got married, and how you could not wait for the ceremony to begin in order to receive from the Lord the gift of the man or woman you married. On the wedding day you saw your spouse as a wonderful gift from God and you were proud to belong to this man or woman. But as life unfolds we let ourselves lose sight of this and other blessings God has given us. We allow careers, children or other interests to take over in our life, and our focus shifts to our own needs and does not stay on the needs of our marriage relationship. Instead of jumping with joy when our husband knocks, we tell him to go away because our bed is too comfortable or we have something more important to do than to attend to him.

The bridegroom's selfless response

The first part of this chapter of the song shows that serious trouble has come into this relationship. This man was looking forward to some attention and appreciation from his wife, for emotional and physical intimacy at the end of his day, but when he knocks at her door he is rebuffed. You can be sure that most men in his place would be angry and feel that they have been wronged and denied something they are entitled to. A man who feels wronged has a tendency to become angry and to retaliate. Again, this is not meant to be seen as a real event but rather as an example of how such a scenario could play out in a marriage relationship. Husbands often retaliate by mistreating their wife as they feel they are being mistreated. A man who is spurned by his wife may simply ignore her or refuse to serve her—if she will not do that for me, then I am not going to do this for her. There are many foolish ways in which we attempt to hurt or get back at our husband or wife, many of them involving behaviour worse than children might use toward one another. At other times we simply go off and sulk, feeling sorry for ourselves. When married couples get into such hurtful patterns of recriminations and self-pity there is a point when it becomes very difficult to work together anymore. Imagine if this man had become angry with his wife and commanded her to open the door for him. She might, in turn, have said, "Do you see why I did not want to get up and open the door for him? If that is the kind of person he is, then I don't want him to come to me." She will feel justified in her actions.

Instead of letting a negative situation develop, however, this man acts wisely and deals with his wife in a loving way. Although he must have been hurt by his wife's actions, he continues to treat her with love and respect. He does not make any further demands on her, but he allows her to enjoy her sleep undisturbed and goes on his way. On the other hand, or maybe because of his wise response, the woman does not feel very good about what she has just done, and she quickly gets up to open the door. When she opens the door she does not see him but finds myrrh, an expensive ointment, on the door lock, and she says, "My hands dripped with myrrh, my fingers with flowing myrrh, on the handles of the lock." There is much discussion about who put the myrrh on the door. Did the woman herself put it there when she went to unlock the door, or did the man leave it behind on the lock of the door? While the original Hebrew words used here can be understood either way, there appears to be no real significance behind the woman leaving the myrrh on the lock. On the other hand, if the husband left myrrh on the lock of the door, he leaves behind a subtle message of love for his wife when she opens it and finds her hand covered with myrrh. We could call it his love letter.[1] It is part of his loving and wise reaction to her response to him. This is how a man must love his wife and how partners in a marriage must respect each other. Although he is called to give leadership as the head of this relationship, that does not give him the right to put all kinds of demands on his wife. A husband is called to love his wife when she treats him well, but to love her also when a difficult situation arises in which she wrongs him. When one spouse in a marriage wrongs the other, it does not give the wronged person the right to retaliate or react in anger. We are always called to respond with love and respect, a tall order and an ideal that husbands and wives often fail to live up to.

The Lord Jesus, however, perfectly measures up to this ideal. Imagine if he was not the perfect bridegroom who loves his bride in all situations. If that were the case, we would constantly be afraid and insecure before him, because we repeatedly grieve him with our selfish attitude. We grieve the Lord through our indifference and unwillingness to sacrifice everything to serve him. We are not always willing to show him the respect he deserves or to submit to his will. Christ would be fully justified in retaliating and withdrawing his love from us, but thankfully our great bridegroom is endlessly patient and loving. He puts up with our weakness out of love, because he has bought us at the cost of his blood. We deserve his anger, but instead he continues to treat us with love and respect, and he constantly reminds us of his love for us through the gospel, which was given to us as a wonderful letter in which he speaks about his great love for us, his bride. We cannot even begin to comprehend the Lord's patience. If he did not treat us with utmost love and respect, we would have been destroyed long ago. Our life is secure in the perfect love of the Lord Jesus.

A husband must treat his wife in the same way Christ treats his bride, the church. Headship is not about controlling and dominating your wife and expecting her to fulfill your needs. Headship is about serving your wife out of love and treating her with great respect. There is never an excuse for failing to love and respect your wife, and no matter how frustrating and disappointing she may be, God has given her to you and you are called to love her with your whole life. That takes great wisdom and patience, but it is the only way that your relationship can grow. When you got married, you did not force your wife to marry you, but she married you because you wooed her with your love. It was your love for her that made her say that she wanted to live the rest of her life in your shelter; she said, "I will marry this man because his banner over me is love." In marriage, you cannot force your wife to love you or serve you, but you must continue to win her with your love.

I sometimes wonder why men and women spend so much energy trying to force or manipulate their spouse into doing their will. How can force or anger ever solve anything in your relationship? How do you expect your wife to follow you when you bully her? How do you expect your spouse to respond to you positively when you manipulate them? Husbands, your wife will only follow you if you love her with your whole life. We follow Christ not because he forces us to but because he loves us and this love creates a fierce loyalty for him in our heart. When a man loves his wife, she will follow him with joy because she knows that he respects her and truly loves her.

Love rekindled

In the myrrh the husband left on the lock of his wife's door we see an important message. She has turned him away, but he still says, "I love you." And when the woman sees that love in his response, her heart immediately goes out to him, because she realizes what she has not loved her husband as he loves her. His love for her kindles a love in her heart for him, causing her to go out right away to look for him when she realizes that he has gone.

As the woman is looking for her husband, she meets the daughters of Jerusalem and asks them to find the one whom she loves. When you find him, she says, "Tell him I am faint with love." They, in turn, want to know what is so special about him that she would ask them to do this for her. She responds with a glowing description of the man that clearly comes from a heart that suddenly remembers everything she loved so dearly about him. She describes and praises his physical attributes in great detail, referring to his complexion, hair, eyes, cheeks, lips, arms, torso, legs and mouth. In her words, he is "outstanding among ten thousand." He is solid and cannot be moved because "his appearance is like Lebanon, choice as its cedars." Her description tells us a number of things about her husband. It gives us a sense of the greatness of this man. The outward physical description of him must reflect the inner beauty and strength that she respects. Instead of eyes that are hard with anger, as they could be after her poor behaviour, he looks at her with eyes that are soft and loving. To her, his mouth is sweetness, and she loves to kiss his lips because those lips did not spout forth angry, hurtful or demeaning words. His words were tender and caring. She loves to live under the shadow of this man. She took his love for granted, but now she recalls why this is the man for her. Her love is rekindled because of the love and kindness he has shown her.

She describes a man who almost seems too good to be true. Is there such a man, such a husband, who meets these high ideals? Of course, the only one who does is Jesus Christ, and the description she gives is fulfilled in the life of Christ. Christ is the one who looks on us with kindly eye and who speaks to us about his love and care. He is the great bridegroom who speaks words of encouragement to us as our head. When you remember what Christ has done for you, how can his love leave your heart untouched? His awesome work for you must rekindle and awaken a great love in you for your Lord.

When you live in his love, his love will also be reflected in your marriage relationship. Do not take the love of your husband or wife for granted, but serve each other out of love, showing great respect for each other. And do not wait until your spouse takes the initiative but be the first to love your spouse. Perhaps much has happened to destroy your love. Maybe things have been said or done to diminish your respect for your spouse, but in the power and love of Christ Jesus you must learn to lay aside your anger and bitterness. When your love for Christ is rekindled, it is also possible to bring love back into your marriage. That love for Christ is the first step for reconciliation; this will become clear in the next chapter. May the marriage the Lord gave you grow and flourish in a way that honours the great bridegroom, Jesus Christ.

For Further Reflection

1. How do you deal with times of conflict in your relationship and how would you change that so that they become opportunities to grow in love and intimacy?
2. Identify the things in your relationship that undermine the love and care you had for each other when you were first married. Discuss how you might deal with the daily stresses of life in a healthy and spiritual manner that protects your love.
3. How important to you is your relationship with Christ? What pressures of life threaten your relationship with him? Discuss what a healthy relationship with Christ looks like.
4. Discuss how it is possible to regain the passion for our spouse that you had on your wedding day.
5. What are some of the hurtful strategies husbands and wives often use with each other? Can you identify ways in which you react to the slights of your spouse?
6. Discuss why the man in this song responds to his wife by leaving myrrh on the handle of the door. How might you respond in similar ways to your spouse?
7. Discuss how Christ's love for us, even though we often hurt him by our selfishness, teaches us how we are to love our spouse.
8. How do you win the love and respect of your spouse? How does Christ win the love and respect of his bride, his people?
9. Discuss why rekindling your love for Christ is necessary for rekindling the love for your spouse.

Chapter 11

Love Seeks Reconciliation

Where has your beloved gone,
most beautiful of women?
Which way did your beloved turn,
that we may look for him with you?

My beloved has gone down to his garden,
to the beds of spices, to browse in the gardens and to gather lilies.
I am my beloved's and my beloved is mine;
he browses among the lilies.

You are as beautiful as Tirzah, my darling,
as lovely as Jerusalem,
as majestic as troops with banners.
Turn your eyes from me; they overwhelm me.
Your hair is like a flock of goats descending from Gilead.
Your teeth are like a flock of sheep coming up from the washing.
Each has its twin, not one of them is missing.
Your temples behind your veil are like the halves of a
pomegranate.
Sixty queens there may be, and eighty concubines, and virgins
beyond number;
but my dove, my perfect one, is unique,
the only daughter of her mother,

> the favorite of the one who bore her.
> The young women saw her and called her blessed;
> the queens and concubines praised her.
> (Song of Songs 6:1–9)

The previous chapter dealt with a conflict that arose in the marriage relationship. This song does not hide the fact that in every marriage there are times when the love between a husband and wife needs to be rekindled. This woman understands that since she has wronged her husband, she cannot just pretend that everything is okay. She is determined to find her husband and restore the relationship. Her love demands that she fully reconcile with him. Such reconciliation is only possible when husband and wife remain fully committed to their marriage vows. While a perfect marriage is impossible because of our sinful inclinations, through Christ a couple can again enjoy a good marriage relationship that honours the Lord. Faithfulness to the marriage vow leads to love that always seeks reconciliation.

Covenant faithfulness

As we learned already, after turning away her husband in 5:3–4, the woman of the song regrets her actions and her heart goes out to him. She rushes to open the door, but it was too late—he is gone. Going into the city to find him, she asks the daughters of Jerusalem for their help. Understandably, they want to know, "Where has your beloved gone, most beautiful of women? Which way did your beloved turn, that we may look for him with you?" We wouldn't expect her to know where her husband has gone; after all, she just asked them to help her find him. Surprisingly then, she says, "I know where my beloved has gone. He has gone down to his garden, to the bed of spices, to browse in the gardens and to gather lilies," a response which at first reading does not make sense to us. This should not surprise us though, as this is a book of poetry, conveying moods and ideas and not a narrative, as we have seen before. Understanding the difference between a narrative and a poem will help us understand the song.

There are two different approaches one could take to understanding this text, and both lead to the same message. On the one hand, by being able to describe where he is, the woman might be saying, "I know that my husband has not deserted me; I know his integrity so I am sure he will be busy looking after our gardens. He has not run off but he is looking out for the welfare of his family." The other approach to the text is more reflective of the poetry in the song. The language she uses in 6:2 to describe where he can be found already appeared earlier in this book, on their wedding night, in the groom's description of his bride as a locked garden. At that point, in 4:16, the bride invited her bridegroom into "his" garden[1] giving herself to him and inviting him to consummate the marriage. In 5:1 the man sings about coming into his garden and the wonderful intimacy they could enjoy as husband and wife. His wife now uses this same language to explain to these women where her husband can be found.

Her description of her husband browsing in his garden and gathering lilies tell us that she is confident of where he can be found. The relationship has been troubled, but still it is as if he never went away. Even though she brought conflict into the relationship by pushing him away with her self-absorbed attitude, he is still faithful to her. He did not abandon her in a fit of anger and he did not try to take revenge on her. She knows her husband and that he is true to the promises he made; he will never abandon his marriage vows by becoming unfaithful to her. This teaches how important the commitment to our marriage relationship really is.

In scripture, the marriage vow is fundamental to every marriage relationship because it is the basis on which the couple builds their life. When a couple makes a vow to each other, they make a commitment to love each other and be faithful to each other for the rest of their lives. Thus, the woman in the song can say to the daughters of Jerusalem that she knows her husband has not abandoned her because he has made a commitment to her. Of course, a vow itself is no guarantee that a spouse will remain faithful; consider that today forty per cent of marriages fail before the thirtieth wedding anniversary. It seems to me that today the vow has lost its value because people are so willing to break their wedding promises when the relationship runs into trouble or it no longer fills their need. As a result, there are many couples today who no longer see any value in making marriage vows in the first place, instead deciding to live in a common-law relationship in which they do not make a lifetime commitment to one another. There may be a romantic notion that their love will last forever even without making a vow to be faithful always.

For the Lord God, marriage involves a covenant bond that should be a reflection of the covenant bond God has with his people. The Lord often complained that his people were adulterous because they had become unfaithful to him by serving other gods. The Lord was grieved because he had entered into a covenant bond in which both he and his people had vowed to be faithful to each other. The Lord expects his people to be faithful to their vows to him, and he likewise demands that they be faithful to the marriage vows they make with their spouse. Therefore, it is important that couples in marriage truly value the vows that they have made to each other before the Lord. A vow is a promise that we keep for life, both in good days and in bad, and God will always hold us accountable to this. The woman of this song is certain her husband is faithful to her, not just because he made a vow, but because she also knew his character and commitment to the Lord. She knew that he would always be true to his vow even when she may have shown a lack of care and concern for him through her own selfishness. Like the man of this song, someone who is true to the Lord will take his or her vow seriously and on that basis a couple can confidently begin married life. Marriage itself will not be an easy road to travel; there will be sacrifices that need to be made to love one another as Christ has loved us, but it is a road that can be travelled joyfully when husband and wife remain faithful to their vows.

Within the security of a covenant bond in which husband and wife make a vow to each other, love has the safe environment that it needs to grow and flourish. The Lord himself recognized the importance of a covenant bond when he drew up the covenant relationship with his people. In that covenant, God makes a vow that he will always remain faithful and maintain his love for us. Thinking about your own relationship with God, have you ever wondered how it is possible to be sure that God loves you? How can God love us when so often we push him away with our sinful and selfish attitudes? And when we push God away in those times of rebellion, how do we know where we can find him again? We know where to find God because he promises in his covenant that he will always be faithful and love us for the sake of Jesus Christ. He promises that he will always be there for us when we turn back to him in faith and true repentance. Since God is always faithful to his promise to care for us, it is possible to live every day secure in his love. Even when I am stubborn and rebellious, the Lord does not push me away but calls me back so that I may live in his love. How can you not love the Lord God whose steadfast love is forever? And therefore we also know where to find God in our daily struggles, because he promised he will hear us when we cry to him in faith. His covenant promise means that we never need to doubt the love of God or the love of our great bridegroom Jesus Christ. As a child of God we can experience a wonderful sense of security because God is faithful to his covenant promises. Our love for God can grow within the security of God's covenant.[2]

The same principle is true in a marriage relationship. Our marriage vow is the foundation the relationship is built on. Love itself is not the foundation, but the foundation is the commitment you make to each other, and it is in this secure environment that the love between you will grow. Even after hurting her husband, the woman in this song knows where he is, and she is sure that he has not left her because he is faithful to his vows. She expresses it clearly in 6:3, "I am my beloved's and my beloved is mine." She also spoke these words before they were married, in 2:16, at which point the "you" and "me" changed to "us." The relationship had then deepened to the point where they were ready to make a lasting commitment to each other in marriage. Now, at this point of conflict in the marriage, she can recall the commitment they made to each other and feel secure about the relationship. She remembers that they belong to each other and that they have made a lifetime commitment, because "I am my beloved's and my beloved is mine." It is clear that a husband and wife who are faithful to their vows do not need to worry about their marriage every time they have an argument or disagreement. When anger sometimes leads to hurtful things being said, this can be weathered because their love is grounded in the vows they have made to each other. But if that was not the case, then every argument, dispute and angry outburst becomes a threat to the marriage.

This woman feels secure knowing that her husband will remain faithful in spite of what she has done to him. As a man of integrity he keeps his word and commitments even though he might be angry and hurt. Therefore, she is sure that he will be in his garden, tending to the beds of spices, browsing in the gardens and gathering the lilies. He will always be there to tend to her needs.

Husbands need to show that sort of strength of character to their wives. Can your wife trust that when you have an argument you will continue to give her your wholehearted commitment? The easiest way to deal with our anger is by throwing in the towel and no longer giving a wholehearted effort to living together in love. A husband may no longer be committed to providing for his family, withholding money for their needs. He may also withhold his affection from his wife or he might not fulfill his role in the household by refusing help with the children or taking care of chores in the home. When bitterness and anger sets into our heart, we are able to find so many ways to undermine our marriage. We may even think that by doing these things we are sending a message to our spouse, but all we are really doing is creating an environment of insecurity in which love cannot function. Wives need to be able to look up to their husbands as men who are faithful to their vows even when conflicts arise. Conflicts and disagreements can never be used as grounds to neglect our responsibilities. We fulfill our responsibilities not because our spouse deserves it but because we are faithful to the vow we have made to them. A man who refuses to fulfill his vow is not worthy to be called the head of his wife. No matter how difficult things may be or how our feelings were hurt, the Lord still calls us to be faithful to the vows we made at our wedding. In Robert Bolt's play *A Man for All Seasons* Thomas More explains to his daughter why he cannot go back on his oath: "When a man makes a promise, Meg, he puts himself into his own hands, like water. And if he opens his fingers to let it out, he need not hope to find himself again." In their book dealing with marriage conflict, Les and Leslie Parrott point out that as human beings we create and define ourselves through our commitments, which become an integral part of our identity (50). To break your commitments is to break who you are.

Sometimes, however, men and women face difficult trials in their marriages, so much so that we wonder whether it is really possible for them to remain faithful to their vows. I have seen many couples struggling mightily in their marriages and becoming exasperated, often declaring, "I can't handle this anymore. I need to get out." In order to help these couples we need to understand the incredible pressures that often overwhelm them and the hopelessness they feel. It is not helpful to tell people that they just need to be strong, because in those times they are not strong and they can't stand on their own. Actually, the only way a couple moves forward in this difficult situation is by understanding that they don't have the strength to do this themselves. It is vitally important at this low point to remember that your marriage vow rests in the vow that the Lord Jesus has made with you. The Lord Jesus enters into a covenant of grace with all those whom he has chosen as his bride. Hebrews 6:13 says that when God made a covenant with Abraham, he did so by swearing in his own name, because there was no greater name than his own. God swore in his covenant that he would never leave or forsake his own, and promised that he would always be faithful and turn everything to our good. If the Lord had not given us this promise, in his own name, where would you find your security today? God's faithfulness never depends on us or on how faithful we are, because there would be no security in that. When we examine our own heart we discover how unfaithful we have been to God. Can you even count the times you have been unfaithful to him? Our sinful nature makes it impossible to offer anything to the Lord that is worthy of his acceptance. And yet, despite our great unfaithfulness, every time we turn to the Lord Jesus in faith we know that he is there, because he has bought us with his blood. As his bride we are so precious to him that he will not walk away from us in anger each time we wrong him, but we may return to him because he remains faithful. We can say the same thing about our relationship with God as the bride of the song says about her husband: "I know that he is mine and I am his." That relationship with Christ is the basis for our marriage relationship as well. If you belong to Christ and believe in his faithfulness to you, then the strength in Christ to remain faithful to your spouse will come to you. If Christ has forgiven you the innumerable times you were unfaithful to him, you will be given the strength to be faithful to your spouse on those occasions when he or she may have caused you sorrow or pain. Your strength to do so rests in Christ.

The situation portrayed in this song reflects the normal troubles that arise in every marriage. But situations can also arise in which one spouse becomes unfaithful to the marriage vow, which has a profound effect on the marriage. The Lord does not demand that a spouse must do everything to maintain the relationship in every situation. In his warning against divorce, the Lord Jesus makes an exception for situations involving marital unfaithfulness (Matthew 5:32). There are also situations in which a spouse is physically or emotionally abusive, making it impossible for the other to continue to live in a proper marriage relationship. No one can or should tolerate an abusive spouse, both for his or her own well-being and for that of the family. In such cases the abusive spouse must be called to repentance, and without repentance and change a marriage relationship is impossible.

Covenant love

In spite of what she has done to him, this man continues to love his wife. In 6:4 he speaks directly to his wife for the first time since he turned away from her door, and he says something that is unexpected: "You are as beautiful as Tirzah, my darling, as lovely as Jerusalem." Think of what we might have expected him to say to her. I think that many husbands would have said something along the lines of, "It's about time to you came!" or "What took you so long?" or some other cutting remark to show their displeasure. It is our sinful nature to protect ourselves from hurt by hurting others in return, and husbands and wives often know exactly how to hurt each other. The sad reality is that by doing so we are undermining our marriage, and the more we hurt one another the more difficult reconciliation becomes.

Conflict arises so very quickly in our relationship, for without thinking we react in a negative way to situations that hurt us. Differences are inevitable between two people with different backgrounds, personalities and ideas. And while conflicts arise spontaneously in a relationship, reconciliation never does. A move toward

143

reconciliation always takes a conscious choice on our part, otherwise it will not happen. For a marriage to work, husbands and wives must make the commitment to do everything necessary to resolve their conflicts, and to never hurt their spouse, never get even with their spouse and never administer the same medicine that was used against them, but instead, with the help of God, each must more and more serve their spouse out of love. When we understand our own weaknesses, we also need to make the commitment that even if our spouse has hurt us or done something to make us angry we will take full responsibility for our own actions against him or her and ask for forgiveness. There needs to be willingness on our part to ask for forgiveness for the hurt that we have caused, and at the same time a willingness to forgive the wrong that was done against us.

That is the attitude that is clearly displayed by the man in this song when he sees his wife again. Before she can say anything about how sorry she is, he says, "You are as beautiful as Tirzah, my darling, as lovely as Jerusalem, as majestic as troops with banners." Notice how he loves her too dearly to allow this conflict to destroy the relationship, and therefore his attitude is one in which he acts as if he cannot even remember what she has done to him. He is just happy to see her. While it would be natural for one spouse to resent the other in this situation, in a healthy marriage, couples learn to be patient with each other and are willing to overlook each other's shortcomings because of the love of our bridegroom, Jesus Christ. Imagine if Jesus Christ withdrew his love and care every time we became unfaithful and hurt him. If that were the case, a relationship with Christ would be impossible, since we hurt and grieve him every day. But Christ looks at us as his bride who has been washed clean from our sins by his blood. That does not mean that Christ ignores our sin, or that he will not become angry with those who stubbornly rebel against him. Outright unfaithfulness and a hardening of the heart in rebellion against Christ will cause him to sever that relationship. The same is true in marriage; when one spouse is unfaithful and refuses to live in the marriage relationship, the marriage bond is broken.

From the exchange between the husband and wife at this point in the song we see actions that mirror how, in our relationship with Christ as our bridegroom, he does not insist on his rights, but he shows patience with us as his bride. Instead of hurting us with harsh words in return when we hurt him, he approaches us with words of endearment, reminding us of how great his love for us really is. That is the way Christ endears himself to us. The same is true in marriage. A husband draws out his wife's love, not by insisting on his rights, but by speaking words of affection and love.

In the words exchanged during this episode in the first verses of chapter 6 of the song we can hear how this man builds his wife up. When he sees her, he does think of how she wronged him, but he only sees the one he loves with his whole heart and who is very special to him. He describes her as being as beautiful as Tirzah, as lovely as Jerusalem. We know very little about the city of Tirzah other than it was the capital city of the northern tribes of Israel for a short period after the reign of Solomon, but we know much more about Jerusalem. He praises the beauty of his wife by comparing her to these two cities in Israel. In 6:5–7 he goes on, using many of the same descriptions for his wife as he used earlier, on their wedding night. He says her hair is like a flock of goats descending from Gilead, her teeth like a flock of sheep coming up from the washing, her temples like the halves of a pomegranate. While these descriptions are not the sort of flattering words we would use, they convey her beauty for the people in that culture.

But there is an important difference between this description and his earlier one in 4:1–7. Speaking to her now, after their conflict, he leaves out the more sensual and sexual language; unlike on their wedding night, he does not make any reference to her lips or breasts. It is clear that he finds her just as physically attractive now as he did on their wedding night, so there must be another reason for this. He says to her in 6:5, "Turn your eyes from me; they overwhelm me," or perhaps better, "lest they arouse me," indicating that he is resisting his physical attraction to her. While trying to understand why he would do or say this, it is important to keep in mind that this is a scene of reconciliation. At this time, the husband's priority is to be reconciled with his wife; it is not to seek an intimate moment with her—that is what was happening in 5:2–3, and which led to the conflict in the first place. Husbands might be tempted to say nice words and make amends only when they seek sexual favours from their wife. But if that is the motive, then reconciliation is not possible. Any wife will see those words for what they really are. What we see in the song, therefore, is that the husband does not want his wife to have any reason to believe that he is only speaking these words because he is looking for a favour from her. Rather, his expression of love comes from the depth of his heart.

The New Testament uses a number of different words for love: one is "eros" and another is "agape." Eros clearly refers to sexual love while agape refers to the heartfelt love and care we have for someone. Christ's love for his bride is agape, a love that conveys a deep heartfelt desire to care for others. It is this love of Christ for us that must be the love we build our marriage on. This love shows genuine care for your spouse, and this is the type of love that this man wanted to convey to his wife at this time. In 6:8–9 he tells her that she is very special to him, using the image of a king who may have sixty queens and eighty concubines and virgins or young maidens beyond number, but none of them compares to her. She is very special in his eyes and he has committed himself to her only. Yes, he was hurt when she refused to open the door for him after he came home late in the evening, but that does not take away his love for her. If anything, it only causes him to open his heart to her even more. Her rejection at that time reminded him how great his love for her really is. Therefore, when he next sees her, he praises her with kind words to let her know how dear she is to his heart.

Is this any different than Christ's relationship to us? His love for us, his bride, was so great that he bought us with his own blood, and therefore it grieves the Lord Jesus deeply when we are unfaithful to him. But Christ does not immediately lash out and hurt us as he justifiably could, and instead the scriptures are full of words of love and encouragement that Christ speaks to his bride the church. How often did Israel rebel against the Lord, and what did the Lord do each time? He wooed his people with his love, as you can read in the book of the prophet Hosea, which can be characterized as God's love letter to Israel. Jesus Christ is the same bridegroom today. He continues to love us even when we do not deserve it. He is compassionate and long-suffering, and full of tender mercy. When you love the Lord with your whole heart, you love him not because he forces you to love him, but because he loved you first. Because of his covenant love that does not depend on our perfect love for him, we may feel secure in the arms of the bridegroom. The question is, how will you respond to the love of Christ? Do you reject his covenant love and ignore his loving care, or will you respond in faith with love? The love of Christ only draws us to love him more.

Just as Christ is compassionate, long-suffering and full of tender mercy, your marriage relationship must reflect the same biblical pattern. A happy and blessed marriage is one that is built on and modelled after the love of Christ. The children in your home should also see Christ's love clearly displayed in the love and devotion that you have for each other. A home where husband and wife are devoted to each other in Christ Jesus is a happy and blessed home where a family finds refuge and experiences what it means to live in the love of Jesus Christ.

For Further Reflection

1. Discuss the importance of a marriage vow in a marriage relationship. Is such a vow really necessary for a stable, long-term marriage? Seeing that so many marriages end in failure, is it realistic to expect a marriage to last a lifetime?
2. Discuss how God's covenant bond with his people should be reflected in the covenant bond between a husband and wife. How does this affect your understanding of the seriousness of the marriage vow and your commitment to your spouse?
3. Why did the woman know where to find her husband? How do we know where to find our bridegroom, Jesus Christ?
4. List some ways in which commitment (and not love) is the foundation for marriage.
5. What are some ways in which you may be sabotaging your own marriage? Do bitterness and anger affect the way you see your spouse? How might you break that destructive pattern in the relationship?
6. How do you encourage a couple who are overwhelmed by troubles in their marriage? On what basis can they hope to move forward in their relationship? How does Christ's relationship with us as his bride become a source of strength for us?
7. Discuss the principle that conflict arises spontaneously but reconciliation never does. How committed are you to making reconciliation an important aspect of your relationship? Are there things for which you need to ask forgiveness and seek reconciliation from your spouse?
8. How is the man's attitude towards his wife an example to us for dealing with our spouses when they have hurt us? How does his action impact the marriage relationship?
9. How does Christ interact with his people when they hurt and grieve him by their actions? How does Christ endear himself to us? How does a husband endear himself to his wife?
10. How does the man in this song speak to his wife so that he builds her up? How do you speak to your wife so you build her up? Why is your motive in speaking flattering words so important to your spouse?

Chapter 12

Joy in Our God-Given Roles

Who is this that appears like the dawn,
fair as the moon, bright as the sun,
majestic as the stars in procession?

I went down to the grove of nut trees
to look at the new growth in the valley,
to see if the vines had budded
or the pomegranates were in bloom.
Before I realized it,
my desire set me among the royal chariots of my people.

Come back, come back, O Shulammite;
come back, come back,
that we may gaze on you!

Why would you gaze on the Shulammite
as on the dance of Mahanaim?
(Song of Songs 6:10–13)

The bride delights in her role

*I*t is difficult to determine the speaker of the words in the opening verse of this section. In the previous verses of this chapter of the song, the husband is describing the great beauty of his wife when, suddenly, here in verse 10 the direct speech changes to indirect speech. One possibility is that the husband is simply quoting what the maidens and queens and concubines are saying about his wife in verse 9. In any case, people looking at this couple see the glory of this woman, and because of this glory they will cry out to her a little later in 6:13, "Come back, come back, that we may gaze on you!" Her glory is described in progressively more brilliant light, as she first appears as a distant and dim light that rises at the dawn. This is another instance of an unfamiliar image that does not allow us to fully appreciate what these words might have conveyed to the ancient reader. She is as fair, or beautiful, as the moon, as bright as the sun and as majestic as the stars in procession. The last part literally says, "She is as awesome as an army with banners." Within the context of the light of the dawn and the moon and sun, it is likely that this army with banners refers to the multitude of stars in the sky. Therefore, the translation—that she is as majestic as the stars in procession—seems to capture the thought well. This woman is described in glowing terms. Her radiance shines forth so that everyone can see her glory. What makes her shine with such radiant glory? This description would not have been very fitting just a few verses earlier, in chapter 5 which describes the tension in the relationship after she made excuses for not greeting her husband at her door during the night. At that time she refused to fulfill her role as his wife by not giving loving support to him. They have since moved on from that conflict and are reconciled. Now that the relationship is restored, everyone can again see her glory in the way she fulfills the role God has given her in her marriage.

Paul writes about the glory of the woman who fulfills her task as a wife to her husband (1 Corinthians 11), a perspective which reflects that of this text.[1] He says in 11:3, "Now I want you to realize that the head of every man is Christ, and the head of the woman is man, and the head of Christ is God." Paul is indicating that God gives different roles to each party in these relationships. A little later, in 11:7, Paul speaks further about the roles God gives, saying about the man, "He is the image and glory of God; but the woman is the glory of man." Notice the wording: "man is the image of God." Paul is not saying that the woman is the image of man, because the woman is as much the image of God as the man is. God said in Genesis 1:26, "Let us make man in our image, in our likeness, and let *them* rule." Clearly, God made them both, man and woman, in his image. Therefore, men and women are equal as image bearers in the eyes of God. In Galatians 3:28 Paul says, there is "neither male nor female, for you are all one in Christ Jesus."

Paul is not arguing in 1 Corinthians 11 that the husband is superior to his wife, but he is indicating that God has given different roles to each of them. While both males and females are made in the image of God, the man is the glory of God and the woman is the glory of man. Before we determine how the woman is the glory of man, we need to understand how man is the glory of God. When God created man in his own image, he gave man the task to have dominion over his creation (Genesis 1:28). When men are faithful in that role, this will reflect on God himself so that God receives the glory. Thus, man reflects the glory of God by faithfully serving in the role God gives to him. We discover the same situation to be true in the relationships within the triune God. When Jesus Christ came to this world, he did not come to reveal his own glory, but he revealed the glory of his Father. Christ did this by fulfilling the role the Father gave him to do; that is, to save his people. In his role as Saviour he glorified his Father.[2] Does the fact that Christ fulfills the role his Father gave him mean he is inferior to his Father? Not at all! In his divine nature Christ is equal to the Father, yet in his role as the Son of God he is willing to submit to the will of his Father, and by doing that he brings glory to the Father.

Understanding the relationship between Christ and his Father helps us to begin to understand what it means that the woman is the glory of man. In Genesis 2:18–24 we read how after forming woman the Lord gave her the role of being a "helper suitable" to her husband. It is clear from the context that a helper suitable is someone like Adam, flesh of his flesh and bone of his bones, and yet one who is different. A helper suitable is someone who can be a companion and is able to support her husband. Earlier in this chapter, God had given man the task to be fruitful and increase in number, to subdue the earth and rule over the creatures, and the task of being stewards of his creation. Some therefore limit the interpretation of the woman's role simply to that of helping the man by bearing children. But the man's role is much larger than producing offspring. He is also to subdue and rule over God's creation, and therefore I believe that the woman's role is to support and assist her husband in fulfilling his mandate to care for God's creation as well.

When wives are faithful in their role of helping and supporting their husbands in fulfilling their role, they bring glory to their husbands just as Christ brought glory to his Father in heaven by being faithful in his role. The same thing can be seen, again, in the relationship between Christ and his church. The church, as the bride of Christ, is meant to be the glory of Christ, and as a church we bring glory to Christ when we fulfil our role as his bride, being faithful to him and submitting our life to his good rule. A faithful church will bring glory to Christ while a disobedient church brings dishonour. Paul's point, therefore, concerning the relationships in marriage, and also the point being made in this song, is that a wife faithfully carrying out her role brings glory to her husband.

In the days of this song already and also today, many men and women do not understand their God-given roles, and the result is that they work against those roles in order to promote their own glory rather than the glory of God through their marriage. A marriage will flounder when a woman does not serve her husband as a suitable helper and when a man does not serve his wife as a proper head. In our culture there seems to be a trend that husbands and wives live parallel lives, each pursuing their own goals at the sacrifice of the marriage relationship. Husbands and wives often pursue different careers with the result that they grow apart. I am not suggesting that spouses should not pursue any of their own interests, but this should never be done at the expense of the marriage relationship.[3] When earlier the woman in this song acted in a selfish way by refusing to fulfill her role toward her husband, it did not make her any happier. This song reveals that it actually took away her happiness; it bothered her conscience and caused her heart to sink into the pit of her stomach (5:6). We read how she felt anxiety, rushing into the streets of the city to look for her husband. The introduction of the watchmen who beat her up (5:7) reveals that there are bad and unhappy consequences when we act in selfish ways, refusing to fulfil the roles that God has given us. There is no joy in marriage when a husband and wife do not serve each other as God intended, each spouse going their own way. This pattern destroys the marriage bond and makes for a living hell. Only when you are faithful to the roles the Lord has given you can your marriage grow and blossom under the blessing of God. That is what is being revealed in this part of the song.

The song also shows us that when this man and woman are reconciled to each other and begin to fulfill their roles again, things begin to change for the better. A marriage that was falling apart is restored and the couple once again experiences joy. The woman is busy again in her task of encouraging and assisting her husband in his work, and the people notice this change, seeing how she stands behind him and assists him. She radiates glory and becomes a shining light in their relationship. As first she appears like the dawn as a dim light, but the light begins to grow stronger, appearing like the moon and then as the sun and majestic like the multitude of stars in the sky. The bride herself becomes a radiant presence.

As the bride of Christ, the church's role and calling represent a similar situation. Paul says that Christ is busy preparing to present his radiant bride, the church, to the Father, without stain or wrinkle or any other blemish, but holy and blameless (Ephesians 5:27). We are called to be that bride of Christ, and it is his desire that we are obedient to him and fulfill our calling as his bride, witnessing to his name and promoting the cause of his kingdom in this world. When you are faithful in that calling, not only will you bring glory to Christ, but you will also become a radiant bride. Then everyone will see that you radiate the glory of Christ. The church that is faithful to her Lord will be a brilliant light as she displays the glory of Christ in this world. In the song, this woman's radiance shines forth in 6:11–12. She says, "I went down to the grove of nut trees to look at the new growth in the valley, to see if the vines had budded or the pomegranates were in blossom."[4] She goes out to find her husband, to be with him, so she can encourage and help him. What had happened earlier in chapter 5 was an event where her life went out of focus for a while as she became absorbed in her own needs. At that time she was looking for what she could get from the marriage and forgot about the role the Lord had given her in it.

The bride exalted by her beloved

This song portrays the woman as the one who has lost her focus and is in need of finding it again while, on the other hand, the man seems to be portrayed as the perfect husband. We know, realistically, that the husband can be just as much at fault for the difficulties in a marriage relationship. By portraying the husband in this way, however, the song appears to foreshadow the perfect bridegroom. In the Old Testament, God often compared his relationship with Israel to that of a marriage.[5] In this relationship, God is always faithful and he keeps all his promises and obligations. God fulfills his role perfectly, but his people Israel often lose their focus and become unfaithful to him. In the New Testament, Jesus Christ appears as the great bridegroom whose attention is always perfectly focused on the needs of his bride, the church. In his great love for the church he laid down his life for her on the cross. That was the unwavering focus in his life. But as the bride of Christ, we struggle to keep our eyes focused on Jesus Christ, quickly losing sight of him when we are captivated by the temptations around us. The scriptures often refer to the world and to the evil one (Satan) as the adulteress who tempts us to betray the Lord.[6] We become unfaithful when we give in to the sinful desires of our heart and pursue the idols and pleasures in the culture around us, refusing to submit to the will of Christ. We cannot give in to the rebellious attitude that lives in our heart, but it needs to be radically cut out of our life. Paul speaks about the need for the circumcision of the heart, making it clear that this is only possible through the power of the Holy Spirit who helps us to overcome our selfish desires (Romans 2:28–29). Therefore, joy never increases when we focus on our own needs and fulfilling our own desires but only as we learn to focus on the Lord Jesus Christ. The more we learn to trust Christ with our whole heart, the greater our joy will be. This joy is possible even in the most difficult moments of our life, for we know that Christ as our bridegroom is faithful and this joy will make us radiant lights in this world.

Without this focus on Jesus Christ it will be impossible for both husbands and wives to fulfill their roles in marriage. It is only in Christ that wives will be able to act as the woman in the song does, going down to the grove of nut trees in order to find her husband so she could assist him with his needs. When she goes, she does so with the intention of checking if the vines have budded and the pomegranates are in bloom, because that is a sign that spring has come. Near the beginning of the song, in 2:11–13, the husband had called the woman to come out with him to see the beauty of the spring, as everything was coming to life. Now she goes out to find him and she looks for signs that spring has come. After being reconciled with her husband, she hopes that spring has returned to their relationship so that everything is new again. She wants their relationship to grow again in intimacy and passion. The previous chapter pointed out the need for commitment in marriage. Commitment to our marriage vows creates the secure environment in which love can grow. But commitment itself is not love. When a husband and wife are truly committed to the relationship, the commitment forms the necessary foundation for their intimacy to grow. And out of that intimacy passion will grow as you learn to truly care for each other from the depths of your heart. This woman is looking for that intimacy and passion when she goes down to the grove of nut trees. It may have been difficult for her to imagine that such love is again possible after what she has done to her beloved, but when she goes to the grove she discovers that spring has indeed returned to the relationship, as can be seen in the subsequent events.

Look at what happens in 6:12, where she says, "Before I realized it, my desire set me among the royal chariots of my people." This is a difficult verse to translate, as the NIV footnote shows, but the sense seems to be clear enough—before she even realizes it, she finds herself with her husband in the royal chariot. In summary, love has blossomed and her husband has forgiven her and gives her an exalted position. He takes her up into his chariot so that all the people can see that they are together again. The people look up to her as if she is now riding with her king. They call out to her in 6:13, "Come back, come back, O Shulammite; come back, come back, that we may gaze on you!" There are many suggestions as to why she is called the Shulammite. Some think it is the feminine form of Solomon's name, as if she is named after Solomon. On the other hand, the definite article before the name indicates it is not her name but that it refers to the place from which she came. We cannot resolve all the issues around this name, but it is clear that this woman is exalted by her husband. Today, it makes us think of the marriage of Kate Middleton and Prince William. His position as future king causes her to become the subject of a lot of interest around the world. People cannot get enough of the image of the prince and his new bride, and they want to see the bride in all her splendour. In the same way, this woman in the song received more than she ever imagined. She wanted love to return to the marriage as if it were spring, and that love brought to her the honour of riding with her husband in his chariot so that she is exalted in the eyes of the people. It was an honour to have such a respected husband.

This reflects the way it is with the church as the bride of Christ. Jesus Christ is our bridegroom who has been exalted by the Father above every name (Philippians 2:9). One day, everyone will bow their knees before him, and the bride of Christ will also share in his exaltation. The church's great joy is that her bridegroom is exalted above the heavens, and the day is coming when we will also be exalted as his bride. One day you will stand with the great bridegroom Jesus Christ at the right hand of God and rule with him over all things. That is the great privilege we may look forward to as the bride of Christ. Therefore, serving the Lord Jesus can never become a burden, for you will find your greatest joy in him. As the bride of Christ we look forward to that day when we will be exalted and everyone will see that we are the glory of Christ. And as we look forward to that day, we may already experience something of that joy in our marriage relationship. When you as husband or wife are faithful to the role that Christ has given you, you may be fully assured that love will blossom like the spring in your relationship and you will be the glory of your Saviour, Jesus Christ.

For Further Reflection

1. What perspective does 1 Corinthians 11 give for the image of the woman who is described in increasingly brighter light (Song of Songs 6:10)?
2. Men and women are both created in the image of God and therefore equal in his eyes, yet the Lord gives different roles to husband and wife. How does the relationship between the three persons in the Godhead (Father, Son, Holy Spirit) reflect this reality?
3. Discuss how a man is the glory of God and a woman the glory of her husband.
4. Discuss how we as the bride of Christ bring glory to his name.
5. Discuss whether our culture today undermines the roles of husband and wife as given by God. When the roles given by God in marriage are undermined, what effect will that have on marriage? What is the blessing in fulfilling the roles God has given to husbands and wives?
6. What does Christ's unwavering focus on his bride teach us about how we are to serve him as our bridegroom? Why is this focus on Christ necessary in order to fulfill our role to our spouse?
7. The woman goes to the grove of nut trees to see if spring has returned. She wants love to blossom again in the relationship. A relationship cannot exist on commitment alone and therefore the woman is looking for passion to return to the relationship. Discuss how you maintain passion in your marriage.
8. Discuss how the bride of Christ will share in the exaltation of her bridegroom. How does this principle present itself in the marriage relationship?

Chapter 13

I Belong to My Beloved, and His Desire is for Me

Come back, come back, O Shulammite;
come back, come back, that we may gaze on you!

Why would you gaze on the Shulammite
as on the dance of Mahanaim?

How beautiful your sandaled feet,
O prince's daughter!
Your graceful legs are like jewels,
the work of an artist's hands.
Your navel is a rounded goblet that never lacks blended wine.
Your waist is a mound of wheat encircled by lilies.
Your breasts are like two fawns, like twin fawns of a gazelle.
Your neck is like an ivory tower.
Your eyes are the pools of Heshbon by the gate of Bath Rabbim.
Your nose is like the tower of Lebanon looking toward Damascus.
Your head crowns you like Mount Carmel.
Your hair is like royal tapestry;
the king is held captive by its tresses.
How beautiful you are and how pleasing,
my love, with your delights!
Your stature is like that of the palm,

and your breasts like clusters of fruit.
I said, "I will climb the palm tree;
I will take hold of its fruit."
May your breasts be like clusters of grapes on the vine,
the fragrance of your breath like apples,
and your mouth like the best wine.
May the wine go straight to my beloved,
flowing gently over lips and teeth.

I belong to my beloved,
and his desire is for me.
(Song of Songs 6:13–7:10)

The idea that a man and woman can be devoted to each other in marriage for their whole lives may seem unrealistic to many. Some argue that since our circumstances and needs in life change over time, you would be foolish to expect a single partner to be able meet those needs. In a certain sense, there appears to be some truth to these sentiments—no one will be able to fulfill every need in the life of their spouse during every stage of life. The reality is that sin has warped and twisted us to such an extent that every marriage relationship feels its negative impact. God himself spoke about this in Genesis 3:16 when he told Eve how the curse of sin would affect her marriage life: "Your desire will be for your husband, and he will rule over you." Because the bond of love is so easily broken by sin it is impossible for anyone to meet all the needs of his or her spouse all of the time. The human solution to the problem of changing needs, to simply leave the spouse for someone else who might meet those new needs, ignores the Lord's purpose for marriage. A biblical understanding of marriage and love teach us that they are never about fulfilling our own needs; they are always about looking out for the needs of others. The same is true in all of our relationships—when we freely give our love to others the Lord blesses it so that it comes back to us. Those who display their love for others will often be surprised by the love they receive in return. On the other hand, if we are only concerned about our own well-being, nothing will ever come back to us. If you do not love others, you will never be loved. This is why the gospel is such a surprise. Jesus Christ reveals his love for his people while they are still enemies of God (Romans 5:10; Colossians 1:21–23). The Lord reveals his love and grace to those who have forfeited everything by their rebellious attitude against him. It is God's love for us that draws us to him. The Song of Songs deals with the restoration of love to what God intended it to be in the beginning. The song reflects on what the love between a husband and wife should really be like. In his grace, God removed the curse of sin for his people so that this man and woman can truly love each other again and joyously express their overwhelming love for each other, the thing which gives them great delight each day.

I belong to my beloved

In the first five verses of chapter 7 of the song, this man gives an intimate description of his wife, and in verses 6–9 he expresses his great desire for her. She responds to these words with great joy in verse 10 when she declares, "I belong to my beloved, and his desire is for me."[1] She continues expressing her desire for him in verses 11–13, and in the first four verses of the next chapter she declares that her desire is to always be able to express her intimate feelings for him wherever they may be. Next, I will focus on the words of 7: 6–9 where the man speaks about his desire for his wife. But in order to appreciate what he says about her, we first need to reflect on what the woman says in 7:10.

There we find her words, "I belong to my beloved, and his desire is for me." We might expect her to say that the man she loves belongs to her, but instead she says that she belongs to him, speaking about herself as his possession. Her words clearly show that this makes her feel secure and extremely happy. In the previous chapter (6:10–13) she went down to the grove of nut trees so see whether love had again blossomed in their marriage. She said in 6:12, "Before I realized it, my desire set me among the royal chariots of my people." She has been faithful in her love for her husband, fulfilling the role that the Lord has given her in their marriage. Some might regard this woman as enslaved in the marriage relationship, but that is not what she experiences. Fulfilling the role the Lord has given her in marriage, she has been given an exalted position in the relationship, making her life much more enjoyable. By living as a wife according to God's plan, she has now become the glory of her husband, the people admire and praise her and she feels a wonderful sense of security. She joyfully exclaims, "I belong to my beloved." Then she adds, "and his desire is for me," which is the real reason for her joy and security. Yes, she belongs to her husband, and yes, in a certain sense she is his possession, but he does not look at her as a piece of property that he can use for his own purpose. Instead, he has set his heart on her and he loves her dearly. He desires her with everything he has. This gives the woman a great sense of security.

What this couple experiences here is true and genuine love, a reversal of the situation after the first man and first woman, Adam and Eve, fell into sin. The word "desire" used by the woman in this song is found in only two other places in the Bible; in Genesis 3:16 and 4:7. In Genesis 3:16, the Lord God came to the woman after she fell into sin and told her how his judgment would affect her life. After telling her that he will greatly increase her pains in childbearing, God says to her, "Your *desire* will be for your husband, and he will rule over you." This is a very different use of the same word from that spoken by the wife here in this song. While some understand the words of Genesis 3:16 in a positive way, God is speaking the words within the context of the judgment he pronounces on the woman for her disobedience. Within this context, her desire for her husband is not healthy desire, but one that is clinging and controlling; it is not the result of love, but the result of necessity.

In a recent conversation with an acquaintance working in the financial services industry, our discussion turned to the vulnerability of widowed women in our society. He observed that all young couples need to have life insurance as no husband should leave his wife and children without arrangements for their economic security in the event of a tragedy. Not doing so might place a mother in a situation where she finds it necessary to marry someone unsuitable out of economic necessity. In his daily work, this financial advisor (from a non-Christian perspective) saw women who cling to men for all the wrong reasons and out of financial need. In my pastoral work I have also seen Christian women persisting in unhealthy relationships.

When a relationship becomes too important for any reason, she can no longer see that the man is unsuitable for her. Maybe he lacks mature spirituality and cannot give spiritual leadership, or maybe in his selfishness he is more concerned about caring for his own needs than for hers. It is not uncommon for both women and men to cling to unhealthy relationships that are a form of slavery and cannot give fulfillment.

God also says to the woman in Genesis 3:16 that as a result of her desire the man will rule over her. In this context of judgment, "rule" must mean that he will oppress his wife by acting somewhat as a dictator over her. A man who rules over his wife in this sense simply uses her to meet his own needs. The reality is that men have dominated women ever since the fall into sin. This was the case not only in many ancient cultures or in more paternalistic societies today, but we even see how in our "liberated" Western culture women are often nothing more than playthings for men. Women may pursue freedom and pride themselves on their independence from men, but their desire for men, for any number of reasons, can cause them to use their bodies to attract attention that is unhealthy or results in dysfunctional relationships. And men use their ability to dominate women to fulfill their lusts and desires. Our modern culture has clearly not been liberated from the judgment that God pronounced on Eve after the fall into sin.

The woman in the song says, "I belong to my beloved, and his desire is for me." While use of the word "desire" here is clearly intended to remind us of God's words of warning to Eve, it also highlights an important difference between what this woman says and what God told Eve. God's words to Eve were, "your desire will be for your husband" but this woman says "his desire is for me." In the Song of Songs, the husband desires the woman rather than the woman desiring the man. Here we have a positive development as this man's love does not allow him to rule over his wife in a domineering way, and he truly desires her for who she is. He does not seek to use her to fulfill his own lusts, but he loves her with his whole heart.

The woman's joyful expression reveals that paradise has been restored to the relationship; that which was broken by sin has been restored in their marriage so that true and genuine love is again possible. She can rejoice again, saying, "I belong to my beloved, I am his possession." I can imagine that many women today would think she must be crazy to say these words; who could possibly want to become the possession of her husband? This woman wants this, because the man she loves desires her. He is not a man who is self-absorbed and only thinking about his own needs, as a relationship with a man like that would become a prison for her. A husband who truly desires his wife and loves her will always take care of her, making her feel secure so that she will experience the greatest joy. True freedom is to be found in a loving relationship between a husband and wife in which a wife feels loved and secure. This man expresses his great desire for his wife in 7:1–9. She is the one on whom he sets his heart.

His desire is for me

At the end of chapter 6, the woman's admirers cry out to her to come back so that they may gaze on her. The response to their cry is, "Why would you gaze on the Shulammite as on the dance of Mahanaim?" The text does not clearly identify who is speaking at this point. Some suggest the husband is speaking and his purpose is to protect his wife from the ogling eyes of the crowd. It seems more likely that the Shulammite woman asks why they would gaze at her. It is also difficult to interpret the meaning of the term "dance of Mahanaim." Mahanaim is the plural form for the term "war camp" and today we do not understand what is meant by the expression, "dance of the war camps." Although we do not understand the expression, it is clear that the young woman does not want to put herself on public display for the entertainment of those who are watching. Her attitude is quite different from that of many who love to suggestively display their bodies to others. These words suggest that this woman has a deep sense of propriety and modesty. The poet may have added this line as an introduction to the next poem where her husband intimately describes her body. This suggests that she will only put her body on display for her husband and not for anyone else. This modesty is something that women need to keep in mind today. Women do not need to be ashamed of their sexuality and they may even enjoy it as a gift, but it is not something that everyone should see. Your body is only for the one you belong to through your marriage commitment and the one who genuinely loves and desires you. Within the marriage relationship you may unashamedly explore your sexuality as if opening your body as a garden of delight to your beloved.

It is appropriate therefore for this woman's husband to gaze at her and admire her physical beauty. He begins describing the beauty of her body in 7:1 with her feet and moves up her body. He has already given an intimate description of her body on the wedding night in chapter 4, and at that time he began the description at her head and worked down her body. There, in 4:1–5, he described seven features of her body but here in 7:1–5 he mentions ten. It has been suggested that since seven is the number used in scripture to describe perfection, the fact that the young man describes seven features of her body shows that he finds his bride to be perfect. By describing ten of her features he declares that he looks at her with still greater delight. While seven is important, ten is even more important, suggesting that things only get better in the marriage relationship after the wedding night (Williamson 62). While we need to be careful in understanding the use of these numbers, the intention of the text is certainly to highlight how this couple's love is intensifying.

With the husband's words describing how beautiful and wonderful his wife is to him, we are coming to the climax of this larger section of the song. He describes her beautiful sandalled feet. The sandal itself accentuates the beauty of her foot, and it is no different today as women look for just the right shoe as the perfect accessory. He describes her graceful legs. More literally, he speaks about her rounded thighs like jewels, which are the work of a craftsman. Her navel is like a rounded goblet that never lacks wine and her waist is like a mound of wheat encircled by lilies. Here he is likely describing the more intimate and sexual parts of her body, as he also does in the next verse when he describes her breasts like two fawns, twins of a gazelle. He says her neck is like an ivory tower, the likely point of comparison being that it is smooth and graceful. He compares her eyes to the pools of Heshbon. It is difficult to exactly catch the mood he wants to create. Perhaps he longs to look into the depth of her eyes as an opening into her soul, like looking into the depths of the pool. And her nose is like the tower of Lebanon looking toward

Damascus. This is not a very flattering description in our culture but it must have conveyed something beautiful in those days. The fact that the tower of Lebanon plays a role in protecting Damascus suggests that it is important. It may simply convey a picture of grandeur. Her head crowns her like Mount Carmel that proudly juts out into the Mediterranean Sea for everyone to look at with wonder. And her hair is like a royal tapestry; literally, it is purple, which is the colour of royalty. Her hair is so beautiful that the king is held captive by its tresses.

This man uses all these descriptions to convey to his wife how beautiful she is in his eyes. Noting how things have only gotten better with time after the wedding of this couple, we can also learn the lesson that romance is important for the marriage relationship, not just for the dating phase. Husbands need to learn from this man the importance of reminding your wife that you truly desire her because she is still beautiful in your eyes. Even though age may spoil outer physical beauty, it is not the outer beauty that matters. We do not fall in love with a body, the appearance of which will change over time, but we fall in love with a person who remains with us for the rest of our married life. Because of this, husbands need to continue to express their love and desire for their wives. Earlier it was said that wives feel secure when their husbands give compliments and speak kind words of endearment to them. This is the way to make it clear that you truly care for your wife and do not take her for granted.

After he describes his wife's beauty, this man moves on to describe his desire for her in 7:6–9: "How beautiful you are and how pleasing, my love, with your delights! Your stature is like that of the palm, and your breasts like clusters of fruit. I said, 'I will climb the palm tree; I will take hold of its fruit.' May your breasts be like clusters of grapes on the vine, the fragrance of your breath like apples, and your mouth like the best wine." It is not necessary to deal with the details of these words because the message is very clear. This man is filled with longing for his wife and the language he uses is explicitly sexual. When he sees his wife and beholds her beauty, his sexual desire for her intensifies. If we were to lift these words out of the context of this song, one might think that this man is overcome with lust. There is often a fine line between genuine desire and lust, but lust is about meeting your own needs and using someone to make that happen while genuine desire for someone is based on a heartfelt love for them. From the way this woman responds in 7:10 it is clear that she does not feel that her husband is motivated by lust but that he genuinely desires her. Her experience is that he truly loves her with his whole heart. If that was not so, she could never say with any joy or conviction, "I belong to my beloved, and his desire is for me."

No man should ever think that simply speaking endearing and flattering words is enough to convey love. Your words need to be genuine and come from the depth of your heart, because a woman will quickly see through empty flattery. You do not, however, need to be a poet like this man in order to show your wife how much you appreciate her, for just some simple, genuine words of appreciation will give her great joy. She needs to hear from your mouth and experience in your actions that you genuinely desire her. If your wife knows that you truly desire her for who she is, she will feel a real sense of security and joy. Her greatest need in the marriage relationship is to be able to joyfully say, "I belong to my beloved, because his desire is for me." When husbands genuinely care for their wives, not only by taking care of their material well-being but also by supporting them in their daily struggles, they will experience a feeling of belonging that gives the greatest happiness.

In our modern culture many think that women are best off when they are not dependent on men for their well-being. For many the ideal is that wives be completely self-sufficient both emotionally as well as economically. There may be a number of reasons for this. Often women have experienced or seen relationships in which a man has been controlling, authoritarian or aggressive. The sad reality is that this kind of behaviour has even been present in "Christian" marriages and it has often been justified as showing proper headship. Such behaviour, however, does not reflect the kind of love Christ shows toward his bride, the church. On the other hand, we also find in our culture that people reject God's intention for marriage, with everyone wanting to assert their own self-sufficiency even when married. The purpose of marriage then is not to become one, but only to enjoy those aspects of the relationship that may be beneficial to oneself. But as was shown earlier, scripture reveals that asserting self-sufficiency in marriage does not give real joy or freedom and it only destroys the marriage relationship. We may find it difficult to understand how this woman's devotion to her husband can be so freeing. We will struggle with this if we do not know the love of Jesus Christ. If you do not know the love of Christ and understand the gospel of salvation it is impossible to give up our desire for such self-sufficiency. This remains a challenge for us as believers because we still struggle with stubborn hearts that rebel against the Lord. We would rather do things our way than God's way, but we will experience the greatest joy only when we know that we belong to Jesus Christ and that Christ's desire is for us.

Thus, we can see that the words the man of the song uses to describe his wife also reflect Christ's words toward those who are his bride. The beauty Christ sees in us his church is not our own natural beauty. It is Christ himself who has made us beautiful again by washing us clean from all our sins with his blood. It is Jesus Christ who clothes us with his righteousness. And because of this gift, when he looks at us as his bride, he sees our new-found beauty and he desires us. Then, because of this we can exclaim with the greatest joy, "I belong to my Saviour Jesus Christ and his desire is for me." My greatest happiness is that I am his possession. When we attempt to live self-sufficient lives without Christ we are totally lost, but in his loving embrace we are totally secure.

That love of Christ is the foundation for the love in your marriage. If Christ can love us even though we are sinners, then in the strength of Jesus Christ a husband can also learn to love his wife despite her many weaknesses and shortcomings. Husbands, each of you can love your wife not because she is perfect but because Christ has given you your wife and he calls you to love her with your whole heart and life. He who first loved you calls you to have a genuine desire for your wife. That desire is to care for her and to give her a safe environment in which she can grow and flourish. When a husband provides a loving environment for his wife to grow and flourish, she will bring glory to him, just as the church brings glory to Jesus Christ when she faithfully serves him out of love.

For Further Reflection

1. Discuss the principle: when you love others you will receive love in return. Are there times when this may not be true? How does this principle function in Christ's relationship with us and do you see evidence of this in your relationship with others and your spouse?
2. Why does the woman rejoice that she belongs to her husband? How is it possible for her to experience this as freedom when today many would consider that she has lost her freedom?
3. Discuss how the woman's words, "his desire is for me," are a reversal of the curse of Genesis 3:16, where God declares that the woman's desire will be for her husband and he will rule over her.
4. What are some kinds of unhealthy relationships that women and men cling to? Discuss some reasons people may do this.
5. We often think women in ancient or paternalistic societies were dominated by men and that women in our Western culture now enjoy freedom. Are there ways in which women in our Western culture still lack true freedom and are being dominated by men?
6. How is the husband's desire for his wife in this song a positive development and one that gives freedom to his wife? How does it reveal that paradise has been restored to the marriage relationship?
7. How does the woman's request to her admirers that they not gaze on her speak about the need for propriety in a modern world that has been so sexualized? What practical implications may this have for your life?
8. Earlier the husband described seven features of his wife's body; now he describes ten. This suggests an intensifying of the couple's love over time. Discuss whether you experience this in your marriage relationship. How can you work on growing closer in love and intimacy?
9. Discuss some of the ways the husband describes his wife and the mood he sets. What is the purpose for this description?

How does it affect his wife? What can a husband today learn from this?

10. The man speaks of his longing for his wife with explicit sexual language. What is the difference between lust and a healthy sexual longing? How does a man convey a genuine desire for his wife so that she experiences it as genuine love?

11. How does the modern concept of self-sufficiency undermine the concept of becoming one in marriage? What does our relationship with Christ teach us about this?

Chapter 14

Mutual Desire

I belong to my beloved,
and his desire is for me.
Come, my beloved, let us go to the countryside,
let us spend the night in the villages.
Let us go early to the vineyards
to see if the vines have budded,
if their blossoms have opened,
and if the pomegranates are in bloom—
there I will give you my love.
The mandrakes send out their fragrance,
and at our door is every delicacy,
both new and old,
that I have stored up for you, my beloved.
If only you were to me like a brother,
who was nursed at my mother's breasts!
Then, if I found you outside,
I would kiss you, and no one would despise me.
I would lead you and bring you to my mother's house—
she who has taught me.
I would give you spiced wine to drink,
the nectar of my pomegranates.
His left arm is under my head
and his right arm embraces me.

Daughters of Jerusalem, I charge you:
Do not arouse or awaken love until it so desires.
(Song of Songs 7:10–8:4)

*A*fter the husband has finished describing the great beauty of his wife, in 7:9 he speaks about his desire to taste her mouth: "May the wine go straight to my lover, flowing gently over lips and teeth." He passionately wants to kiss the lips of the woman he loves so that he might become intoxicated with the wine of her mouth. The woman responds with the words of 7:10, "I belong to my beloved, and his desire is for me," and then she commands him in 7:11, "Come, my beloved, let us go to the countryside, let us spend the night in the villages. Let us go early to the vineyards to see if the vines have budded, if their blossoms have opened, and if the pomegranates are in bloom—there I will give you my love." Her words are similar to those he had spoken in 2:10 when he came to her home. Then, with the words, "Arise, my darling," he had encouraged her to come out with him since the winter was gone and spring was coming. He invited her to come and see the early signs of spring, when the fig trees form their early fruit and the blossoming vines spread their fragrance. In both of these references to spring, that season symbolizes the awakening of love between the young man and woman. In this chapter, the woman responds to the man by suggesting that he come with her into the countryside to spend the night in the villages. She wants to go with him to the vineyards to see if the vines have budded, if the blossoms have opened and if the pomegranates are in bloom. She commands him to discover with her the signs that spring has come and that love has indeed blossomed in their relationship. She promises him that if he comes with her to the vineyards, she will give him her love there. Earlier, she used the vineyard as a metaphor for her own body (1:6) when she said that she had neglected herself. In this instance, when she commands him to come with her to the vineyards, she is telling her beloved that she is ready to give herself to him. She no longer has any reservations and will therefore give him her undivided love, which includes her body and everything that she has. It is significant that the woman takes the initiative and gives herself to her beloved. She feels freedom and security that allow her to give everything to this man who genuinely loves her.

She adds in 7:13, "The mandrakes send out their fragrance, and at our door is every delicacy, both new and old, that I have stored up for you, my beloved." In the ancient world, mandrakes were considered an aphrodisiac. She collected mandrakes but she has also built up a collection of other delicious things, suggesting that she has stored all kinds of fruit and food at the door of their home in order to satisfy him. She may even be saying that when he comes into her vineyard he will find everything he needs to satisfy himself. She wants to be a source of great delight and pleasure to him, and her greatest joy is to satisfy all his needs. Therefore, she tells him to come and she will give him her love and satisfy all his desires.

Then, in 8:1 there is a shift in thought, when she says to her husband, "If only you were to me like a brother, who nursed at my mother's breasts! Then, if I found you outside, I would kiss you, and no one would despise me." It seems rather strange that she would suddenly speak about her husband being like a brother as this does not fit within the image of the romantic relationship being depicted. One explanation for this seeming change in direction could be our own lack of familiarity with the culture at the time of this song. Couples of that era might not have been allowed to engage in public displays of affection for each other while family members were. The point of her comment is that if he were like a brother to her she would be able to kiss him if she met him in public, without being judged by anyone. One might have been able to kiss a brother or sister without anyone thinking anything of it, but to act in the same way with a boyfriend or girlfriend or even with a husband or wife might not have been appropriate. What is clear is that, because of her love, this woman declares a desire to show him her affection wherever they may be.

She next says, in 8:2, "I would lead you and bring you to my mother's house—she who has taught me. I would give you spiced wine to drink, the nectar of my pomegranates." Earlier, in 3:1–4, the young woman had gone out into the city to search for him, and when she had found him she brought him to her mother's house. On that occasion their relationship became public, and they became engaged. But here she wants to take him to her mother's house so that they might enjoy a romantic encounter. The significance of taking him to her mother's house is unclear, but when she says that her mother taught her she is likely saying that her mother has taught her about the ways of a man and the art of intimacy. In her mother's house she would satisfy him with spiced wine to drink and the nectar of her pomegranates. The allusion here is that her beloved will be sexually satisfied as she gives him her body as the cistern from which he may drink for his whole life.[1]

In the end of this section, she finds herself in the embrace of her beloved: "His left arm is under my head and his right arm embraces me." She feels completely secure in his arms because there she knows she is truly loved. In these verses, the woman has revealed her desire for intimacy with the one she loves. She always longs to give him her deepest affection and to live in the loving and secure embrace of his arms.

Love and sexuality

Someone asked me an interesting question about the language that is used in this song. They wondered, if the intention of this song is to express the character of true love, then why is that message conveyed with such explicit sexual language? What is the connection between genuine love and sexuality? Does the explicit language of the song perhaps undermine the message of genuine love?

Over the course of history, there have been periods when the church took the perspective that sexuality was something very separate from love. An allegorical approach to this song in the Old Testament period understood the song to reflect the love between God and his people Israel, and in the New Testament era it was often understood to only reflect the love of Christ for his church. Love was thought to be good, and sexuality considered dirty or at best a necessity tolerated only for the sake of procreation. But this allegorical approach does not account for the explicitly sexual language used by the song's writer and included by the Lord in his holy word. It also encourages a separation between physical and the spiritual matters so that we think the spiritual part of our life is more important than the physical. However, the language and images of this song remind us that everything God has created, including human sexuality, is good and beautiful.

In the words of the song we see that love is not just experienced on a spiritual level, but in marriage a man and woman also experience their love for each other on a sexual level. God reveals that when a man and a woman fall in love, it is natural for them to desire to express that love in a sexual way because that is the way God created us, and that is why the man and woman in this song speak as they do. The intimate, sexual contact between a husband and wife is the deepest expression of their love because this is a physical intimacy they do not share with anyone else. Understanding sexual intimacy in this way we can see how adultery rips apart the relationship at it deepest level. It is a betrayal that tears at the heart of one's spouse. Partners in a marriage have to be careful to reserve their sexual desire for their spouse and not allow it to draw them toward others. The Lord Jesus warns against improper lust of the heart when he says, "If you look at a woman lustfully you have committed adultery with her in your heart" (Matthew 5:28). Men in particular, but women also, struggle with lust and there is plenty of opportunity in today's culture to fall into temptation. But our sexuality is important in the marriage relationship and we need to understand that a real, satisfying sexual intimacy as God intended it is only possible where there is true and genuine love between husband and wife.

Freedom to grow

The opening words of this section reveal another element of how love should function within a loving marriage relationship. In 7:10 the woman says that she belongs to her beloved, and immediately she follows this in 7:11 with a command that he should come with her to the countryside to see the vineyards. The initiative the woman takes in this verse suggests that even though she has submitted herself to her husband by entering into marriage she still feels free enough to command him to come out with her to the countryside. This is one of the great paradoxes of life. She submits herself in love to this man, which leads not to less but to greater freedom in the relationship. Her words are an expression of the joy that this relationship has given her. It is not God's intention that a wife should be dominated or controlled by her husband, but there must always be a mutual respect for one another. It is important to keep this in mind when the apostle Peter much later speaks about how women of the past who put their hope in God used to make themselves beautiful by being submissive to their own husbands, like Sarah who obeyed Abraham and called him her master (1 Peter 3:5–6).

It may seem to the modern reader that Peter's description of a wife's role is in conflict with the experience of the woman in this song. This may partly be due to the negative connotation attached to the word "submission" in our culture. Submission for the modern reader suggests a loss of freedom in which one is forced to meekly fulfill the demands of the other. Paul gives greater insight into the marriage relationship in Ephesians 5:22–33 when he compares it to our relationship with Christ. He says wives are to submit to their husbands as to the Lord and that the husband is the head of his wife as Christ is the head of his church. Paul teaches that in marriage the Lord gave the husband a role that is different from the one he gave to the wife. It is important to note that Paul begins in Ephesians 5:21 by speaking about the need for mutual submission between husband and wife before writing about the different roles each have been given in the marriage relationship. The husband whose role is to act as the head of his wife may not use his authority to force his will on her and act as a dictator, but he is called by Christ to love his wife and to serve her just as Christ sacrificed everything to serve his bride, the church. And the role of the wife is to serve her husband in everything, just as the church serves Christ as his bride. When the husband uses his authority to serve his wife, being willing to sacrifice everything to care for her well-being, and the wife submits to her husband by looking out for his well-being it will lead to great joy in the relationship. This is mutual submission in which a husband and wife use their roles to serve each other and it creates a safe environment in which their love for each other will grow.

When a husband genuinely loves his wife, he will not have any desire to enslave her or manipulate her into doing his will. A husband who fulfills the role given by the Lord understands that he must give his wife both the space and freedom to develop her own talents and abilities. Commenting on this song, Tommy Nelson writes, "A person who receives unconditional love, appreciation, respect, and tenderness at home is going to give the same things to others" (175). A man who is authoritative or domineering creates a toxic environment for his wife, but a man who unconditionally loves his wife and shows appreciation, respect and tenderness for her will provide the conditions for love to blossom. In such a loving and caring environment she is able to develop her talents for the well-being of her husband and family.

Proverbs 31 gives a wonderful example of this in the portrayal of the wife of noble character (Williamson 64). Verse 11 of that chapter of Proverbs pictures a husband who has full confidence in his wife. She brings him good, not harm, all the days of her life. He gives her freedom to run her household so that she selects wool and flax and works with eager hands to make it into clothing. She imports her food from faraway places so that they eat exotic foods. She provides for the needs of her family as well as those of the servant girls who live in the household. She even has the freedom to make economic decisions for the household when she considers a field and buys it. From her earnings she plants a vineyard in the field and she trades her goods for profit. Not only does she provide clothing and food for her children, she even extends her hands to those who are needy. In the end, her children call her blessed, her husband praises her and she receives praise from the people at the city gate.

In the same way that the woman in Proverbs 31 takes the initiative in caring for the needs of her husband and family, the woman in the Song of Songs also feels the freedom to take the initiative in her relationship. She does not use her freedom to fulfill her own agenda but to promote the honour of her beloved husband and the well-being of her family. Every marriage involves sacrifices on the part of both husband and wife. Husbands are called to show leadership by giving support and encouragement to their wives, and wives are called to provide care and support for their husbands. In this part of the song the woman takes the initiative and encourages her husband by calling him to come out with her to the countryside to enjoy a time of intimacy. This song shows us that wives can take the initiative and build up their husbands so that they can function well in the calling God gives them. When wives support their husbands they bring praise upon themselves. Both husbands and wives have the ability to encourage or discourage their spouse. The book of Proverbs reveals that a woman who does not take her role seriously is tearing down her own home and family. Proverbs 14:1 says, "The wise woman builds her house, but with her own hands the foolish one tears hers down." This woman in the song has embraced the role the Lord has given her in her marriage. Feeling secure in her husband's love she encourages him and builds him up. She nourishes him with her love. The result is that the glory of her husband will now be reflected in her.

The same principle holds for the church of Christ. When the church only seeks its own glory and only promotes its own agenda it loses influence in this world. But when the church as the bride of Christ faithfully serves her Lord by faithfully witnessing to his name and submitting to his will, then Christ's reputation is promoted in this world. As the church builds up Christ's reputation in faithful service to him, Christ in turn will promote the reputation of his church. When the church is faithful in serving Christ, she will become a shining light in this world and Jesus Christ will receive all the glory.

Warning about love

After drawing her husband toward an intimate encounter, the woman ends this section in 8:4 by repeating, yet again, the warning to the daughters of Jerusalem: "Daughters of Jerusalem, I charge you: Do not arouse or awaken love until it so desires." She shortens the refrain by leaving out the oath and by doing so her words become more powerful (see 2:7; 3:5). After her own description of her deep and passionate love for her beloved, why would she warn the daughters of Jerusalem against awakening or arousing love? Does she not want these girls to experience such love? She is warning them about the powerful effect that love can have on them. Love is a force that can overwhelm the senses. When someone "falls in love" or feels "love" for someone, all reason goes out of the window. It is a powerful emotion that can make it difficult to make rational decisions and sometimes results in decisions that are later a cause for regret.

The woman is effectively warning them to not grasp at anything that may look or feel like love, but rather to wait for genuine love with a man who truly loves them in return and who knows what genuine love is. The genuine love that this woman refers to can only be experienced through the love of Jesus Christ, so her advice is to not awake or arouse love until you know a man whose dependence on Christ will lead him to love you as Christ loves you. On the basis of such a love you can respond with your love and give your whole life to him, in the same way that you give your whole life to Jesus Christ as your bridegroom.

For Further Reflection

1. What is the woman's intention when she invites her husband to come out with her to the vineyards to see if the vines have budded? How is that being reflected in your relationship?

2. For the second time in the song the woman takes her beloved to her mother's home. What is her purpose in doing so this time? What message does she convey to him and what does this say about your relationship?

3. Discuss the connection between love and sexuality. Does the sexual language of the song undermine the message of genuine love?

4. It seems counterintuitive in our culture that by submitting to her husband this woman experiences greater freedom. How is the concept of submission in scripture different from the idea of being dominated or controlled? How is this concept reflected in our relationship with Christ?

5. Discuss how Paul understands the roles of husband and wife in Ephesians 5. How is the husband to fulfill his role as the head of his wife?

6. How does Proverbs 31 portray a husband who has full confidence in his wife? Discuss the freedom this woman has to fulfill her role in the marriage relationship.

7. How does this woman take the initiative to build up her husband? Discuss how wives are able to encourage their husbands. What initiatives can the bride of Christ take to build up Christ's reputation in the world?

8. Why is another warning to the daughters of Jerusalem necessary? What kind of power does the feeling of love have over people? How can those emotions be a force either for good or bad?

Chapter 15

Living in the Security of Love

Who is this coming up from the wilderness
leaning on her beloved?
Under the apple tree I roused you;
there your mother conceived you,
there she who was in labor gave you birth.
Place me like a seal over your heart,
like a seal on your arm;
for love is as strong as death,
its jealousy unyielding as the grave.
It burns like blazing fire,
like a mighty flame.
Many waters cannot quench love;
rivers cannot sweep it away.
If one were to give all the wealth of one's house for love,
it would be utterly scorned.
(Song of Songs 8:5–7)

The familiar refrain "daughters of Jerusalem" in 8:4 marked the end of another section and prepares the reader for the conclusion of the song. Here, many of the themes presented earlier in the song return as the poet makes some concluding remarks about love. For that reason, 8:5–7 is often considered to be the high point of the Song of Songs as the poet takes a step back to reflect on the nature of love itself. When God created mankind in the beginning, he intended that they should live in a loving relationship both with him and with their fellow human beings. When there is a loving relationship people feel secure, but when sin entered into the world the resulting hatred, anger and evil brought about insecurity. This song reveals that God makes it possible for his people to again enjoy security in a loving relationship.

The words of this song give an Old Testament background for Paul's teaching in 1 Corinthians 13 about the central importance of love in the life of God's people. Paul says, "love never fails," and "the greatest of these is love," and he encourages us to "follow the way of love" (1 Corinthians 13:8, 13; 14:1). But how can love function in a world where humanity has fallen into sin and where selfishness has become the motive of all human beings? How can there be lasting and sacrificial love in a world that is completely broken because of rebellion against God? Paul's conclusion is that we can love again because Jesus Christ in his great love gave his life for us. We can love because God first loved us (1 John 4:19). Christ's sacrifice is the greatest expression of love in this world, and his love is the basis on which we can again love one another.

Love is giving

"Who is this coming up from the desert leaning on her beloved?" The woman in 8:5 leans against her husband as they walk up from the desert and stop under the apple tree where they enjoy a time of intimacy. The image of a desert is used to introduce a new scene in the song. It represents an empty space offering a point from which the poet can build a new backdrop for this couple. In many of the transitions between themes in this song the author marks the change by using a change in the scenery. But one difference between this and other transitions is that here the couple is together as they enter the new scene; in each of the others there has been a physical distance between the man and woman at the outset, before they begin to move towards each other in love. The fact that in this "final scene" they are together from the beginning indicates that they are now together in a marriage relationship. The fact that the woman is leaning on her beloved brings to mind an image of a couple in love. We often see couples in this pose, with the woman leaning against the man she loves, while he might have his arm around her in a protective and possessive way. The image portrays a sense of the intimacy and mutual dependence that the couple feels. They want to be close together as they look to each other for support. They find joy in their relationship and have discovered security in their love for each other. In our text, because of her joy and sense of security, she can say to the man she loves, "Under the apple tree I roused you; there your mother conceived you, there she who was in labour gave you birth."

In this particular context the woman is doing more than just waking her beloved from sleep, for she wakes him up in order to enjoy a moment of intimacy under the apple tree. The fact that this event takes place under an apple tree alludes to a sexual encounter between them, as apples have long been a symbol of sexual desire and fertility (Longman 208). More importantly, it reminds the reader of 2:3 where the woman describes her beloved as an apple tree standing out among the other trees of the forest. Of all the trees, to her he was the most attractive and therefore she said, "I delight to sit in his shade and his fruit is sweet to my taste."

This image of the woman arousing her beloved under the apple tree indicates her longing for intimacy, but there is also another motive for her actions. She reminds him, "Under this apple tree, your mother conceived you, there she who was in labour gave you birth." She rouses her husband under the very same apple tree where his mother seduced his father; where he was conceived and born. It is interesting that she would point out to the man she loves and wishes to seduce that they are in the same spot where his mother seduced his father. A reminder that his parents engaged in a romantic encounter under this same tree may seem to us to be a sure way to destroy the romantic moment for them. But this observation seems to demonstrate that she understands that their love for each other cannot be self-serving, but that it must be seen as part of the larger context of their role in this life. Life passes on through the generations, and looking back she remembers how her husband was conceived in another, earlier loving marriage relationship. Because of his parents' love she is now able to enjoy a loving relationship with him, and the same will be true for the generations that may follow from them.

Looking at the larger purpose of life, these words seem to point quite naturally to a desire for children. Seeing their own relationship in the context of serving a larger purpose, God's purpose, demonstrates a perspective on relationships that is quite different from one that may live in our own hearts and that is often reflected in our society. It is easy to consider our own goals first—career, economic status, pleasure—and children might get in the way of those dreams. When we only look at children from that perspective, they are quickly perceived as more of a burden than a blessing from the Lord (see Psalms 127 and 128).

After the poet has through the course of the song taken the reader through the early stages and development of the love relationship and marriage, with all of the difficulties that often arise, at the end of the song he also reveals how such a loving relationship fits within the context of God's redeeming work. God's work will progress through the generations, and marriage relationships play a role in that. There is a connection here to God's mandate at the beginning in Genesis 1:28, to be fruitful and multiply and fill the earth. In a loving relationship, husband and wife will realize that the Lord has given them a larger role in his kingdom work, and their love for each other will lead to a desire to fulfill that role. Children have an important place in the coming of God's kingdom, because it is through the generations that the Lord will complete and finish his work of redemption. When God's work is complete, the Lord Jesus will return from heaven to establish the glorious kingdom of God.

Love is unbreakable

The reference to generations also gives us some context with which to view the lines that follow. In her passion, the woman exclaims, "Place me like a seal over your heart, like a seal on your arm." In the ancient Near East a seal was an impression in clay or wax made with a stamp that bore a mark serving as a person's signature. She, in effect, is asking her beloved to figuratively place her as a seal over his heart, as a mark of ownership. She makes clear that she is not willing to share him with anyone else and, therefore, she wants him to put her mark on his heart. She reinforces that thought in verse 11 where she says that she does not want to be like one of Solomon's wives who had to share him with other wives.

We have seen already how to some degree this couple's relationship reflects God's relationship with his people. When the Lord entered into a relationship with Israel he made a covenant with them by commanding the people to mark each baby boy at eight days of age with the seal of circumcision.[1] With this seal of circumcision God claimed the people of Israel as his own. In the New Testament, baptism became the seal by which God claims his people as his own. When God places his seal on us he demands an exclusive relationship, one in which we are to love him with our whole heart and always remain loyal and faithful to him. At the same time, God's seal is his guarantee that his bond of love for us will never be broken.

This woman's desire for him to place her as a seal on his heart to guarantee his love is followed by her description of the unbreakable nature of this bond of love: "Love is as strong as death, its jealousy unyielding as the grave. It burns like blazing fire, like a mighty flame. Many waters cannot quench love; rivers cannot wash it away." In the ancient Near East, the words "death," "grave" and "flame" were used as names for powerful mythological gods, and these images describing the power of death would not be lost on the ancient reader or hearer of the song. Even for the faithful in Israel who have a completely different worldview, the image of death is one of finality, because death will never give back those who have died. Death can never be overcome or broken. Jealousy is mentioned also, and it is always associated with love because love is an exclusive relationship, and jealousy arises from the presence of anything that is a rival to it or threatens the relationship. Jealousy can be a destructive force, but scripture also speaks about it in a positive way. God is a jealous God, not tolerating anything that stands in the way of our relationship with him, but in his jealousy he always protects his relationship with his people. Jealousy also causes a husband or wife to stand up and defend their relationship against any rival that threatens it. Jealousy can be so strong that it will never let go of the one it loves. Love is a powerful bond.

Love also burns like blazing fire or a mighty flame once it has been lit, an image that gives a sense of the great power of love. The Hebrew word for flame ends with the same letters that make up the short form for the name of Israel's covenant God: Yah. While this word could be translated "flame of Yah," here *yah* functions as a superlative to emphasize its strength. The use of *yah* also suggests that love is being compared to the might of God, again emphasizing how very powerful it is. In fact, the woman says, "Many rivers cannot quench love." The power of mighty rivers is well known. Living near the mountains in British Columbia, we saw the power of the streams of water that came rushing down the mountainsides in the rainy season, sometimes carrying along huge boulders and washing out highways. Great rushing waters have a tremendous force that washes away everything in their way, but they cannot quench love or wash it away. Love is a great mystery that no one can fully comprehend, but without love, life in this world is impossible. Where hatred and anger reign, it creates a hell, but where there is love there is peace and security. Love is fundamental for the existence of mankind.

If the woman is right in declaring that love is really that strong and powerful, why do so many marriages end in divorce? Why does the love between so many married couples turn to hatred and contempt? Why, in our own relationships, do we so often hurt our spouse by lashing out against him or her? The effect of sin is that we no longer act out of love but out of our own selfish desires. That is why this world could never survive if God did not intervene and reveal his love in Jesus Christ.

The love this woman speaks about is a love that is created and exemplified by God. In the Old Testament, God reveals his love for the people of Israel, delivering them out of slavery in Egypt and even when they rebelled against him in the wilderness on their way to the Promised Land, the Lord in his great love protected them and gave them food to eat and water to drink. And when Israel became unfaithful to God in the days of the prophet Hosea, the Lord in his great love continued to call his people to return to him. Despite their disobedience, the Lord cared so deeply for them that he sent his own Son to save them, and the Lord Jesus in his great love willingly gave his life on the cross for them. God's love for us is so great that it can never be broken. In Romans 8:39 Paul rejoices, saying that there is nothing that is "able to separate us from the love of God that is in Christ Jesus our Lord." Our security rests in the great love God has revealed to us in Jesus Christ. If God has bought you with the blood of Jesus, then there is nothing that can separate you from his love. God's love is as strong as death, his jealousy as unyielding as the grave and his love for us burns like blazing fire. A mighty flame and many waters cannot quench his love and rivers cannot wash it away. True joy and lasting peace and security can only be experienced in the love of God that is revealed to us in Christ Jesus.

This is the security and peace the woman in the song is looking for when she asks the man she loves to make her a seal over his heart and on his arm. She asks him to enter into a bond of love that can never be broken. And this man can give her that security only because he knows the love of God. A husband can truly love his wife only when he first experiences his own security in God's love for him. There will be many challenges to loving your spouse. You still have to face those miserable foxes that get in the way of your relationship. But when you know the love of God in Christ, his love will give you the strength to move forward in your relationship. In Christ you will find the strength to love your spouse and to provide a secure environment in which each of you can flourish. Such love is a powerful love that cannot be broken, for you are standing firm in the love of Jesus Christ.

Love freely given

The woman says at the end of 8:7, "If one were to give all the wealth of his house for love, it would be utterly scorned." You can buy such things as gold, silver and food but you cannot buy love. Money cannot buy loyalty or love and still people attempt to do it all the time. Parents try to buy the love of their children using money, gifts and toys; husbands try to appease their wives with flowers or jewellery. Rich men buy trophy wives, but they cannot buy their love. The reality is that love cannot be bought but it must be freely given. Love is a matter of the heart and any attempt to buy love only cheapens it, because it undermines who we are as people and dehumanizes us, as if we were a commodity to be bought and sold.

This woman gives her love to this man with a willing and joyful heart and she asks him to respond by freely giving himself to her by placing her as a seal over his heart. This exchange of love and commitment wonderfully reflects our relationship with the Lord. In the Old Testament, God freely gave his love to the Israelites. They did not earn God's love through their good deeds, neither were they more worthy than other people, but God in his compassion chose them as his very own. God freely gave himself to them, and in his love he delivered them out of Egypt and gave them Canaan as their own land (Deuteronomy 7:6–9).

Today, the Lord reveals his love in an even greater way by giving us his Son, Jesus Christ. God's love is freely given to everyone who repents and seeks his grace. In his teaching, Jesus clearly revealed that God's love cannot be bought or earned.[2] Jesus says in Revelation 21:6, "To him who is thirsty I will give to drink without cost from the spring of the water of life." When you understand that the love of God is freely given, the only proper response is to love God for his wonderful grace. It is our greatest joy when we are assured in our hearts that there is nothing that can separate us from the love of God in Christ Jesus. This love that God freely gives is the only basis on which we can love one another. When we experience the love of God that cannot be broken and endures forever, it gives us the strength to freely love our spouse. Even when the little foxes threaten your relationship or when your spouse may be difficult to deal with, you can continue to freely express your love for him or her. If God can do that for me, then I, a sinner, can do that for my husband or my wife. Love that is based on the love of God is as strong as death, its jealousy is as unyielding as the grave and it will burn like a blazing fire. Mighty waters cannot quench it and rivers cannot wash it away.

For Further Reflection

1. Discuss how these words form the Old Testament background for Paul's comments in 1 Corinthians 13. What is the New Testament perspective that Paul gives?

2. What is the purpose of the imagery of the woman seducing her husband under the same apple tree where he was conceived? How does this imagery serve to point to the larger purpose this couple has in the service of God's kingdom? How does this determine the attitude in your own relationship, especially in light of the expectations of modern society? What are the priorities for your relationship?

3. What is the significance of the woman asking her husband to place her as a seal on his heart? Is this reflected in God's relationship with his people?

4. How does the comparison of love to death, grave, flame and water speak about the power of love? If love is indeed so powerful, why do so many struggle in their marriage relationship? Why is it necessary for God to intervene in this world with his love and how does his love in Christ give spouses the strength to continue to love one another?

5. Why is it impossible to buy love and loyalty? What are some ways in which you may still attempt to do so? Does this explain why we cannot buy God's love but it must be freely given?

Chapter 16

A Love That Does Not Grow Cold

We have a little sister,
and her breasts are not yet grown.
What shall we do for our sister
on the day she is spoken for?
If she is a wall,
we will build towers of silver on her.
If she is a door,
we will enclose her with panels of cedar.

I am a wall, and my breasts are like towers.
Thus I have become in his eyes
like one bringing contentment.

Solomon had a vineyard in Baal Hamon;
he let out his vineyard to tenants.
Each was to bring for its fruit a thousand shekels of silver.
But my own vineyard is mine to give;
the thousand shekels are for you, O Solomon,
and two hundred are for those who tend its fruit.

You who dwell in the gardens with friends in attendance,
let me hear your voice!
Come away, my beloved,

189

and be like a gazelle
or like a young stag
on the spice-laden mountains.
(Song of Songs 8:8–14)

*T*he Song of Songs concludes with a number of important principles about love that may either seem quaint or strange according to modern social standards and therefore are ridiculed by many. The Lord Jesus warned that the important principles of love would be undermined by society when he said in Matthew 24:12, "Because of the increase of wickedness, the love of most will grow cold." In the last days,[1] Jesus warns, many will turn away from God so that people will no longer love the Lord or their neighbour. Christ does not present a completely new idea in that text as his words reflect what is already found in this song. When people no longer have love for God, then all that is left is self-love. The love of self always causes an individual to put his or her own needs above the needs of others and to use others for their own selfish purposes. In contrast to that, love that does not grow cold is a love that is always self-giving, like the love of Jesus Christ who completely gave himself to his bride, the church. When you live in the love of Christ, the desire of your heart is to love God and your neighbour.

Keeping yourself for the one you love

The brothers first mentioned in 1:6 reappear here at the end of the song where the poet hears them say, "We have a young sister." It is possible that the woman is quoting what her brothers have said about her and that they are offering an opinion about their sister, allowing the poet to examine another aspect about the true character of love. They say, "We have a young sister, and her breasts are not yet grown. What shall we do for our sister for the day she is spoken for?" This takes us back to a time before this woman had matured, since her breasts are not yet fully grown. At that time the brothers were already concerned about her future when she will be spoken for in marriage. As brothers, they take on the responsibility of protecting her for her wedding day, something that was not uncommon in the ancient Near

East, as we can see in the action of Jacob's sons in Genesis 34 against the men of Shechem when their sister Dinah had been defiled.

In this song the brothers indicate their sense of responsibility for their sister's reputation when they say, "If she is a wall, we will build towers of silver on her. If she is a door, we will enclose her with panels of cedar." A wall is erected to keep people out of a city, while a door or gate is the means by which people enter into the city. With these images the brothers express their concern and what they intend to do with regard to their sister's sexual purity. They say, in effect, that if she acts like a wall by keeping herself sexually pure, then they will act as additional protective support for her. "Towers" refer to stone walls built around a camp to protect it from enemies. They promise to reinforce her efforts to remain pure and chaste. They will build these towers (literally, stone walls) using silver to honour her for her chaste behaviour. On the other hand, if she behaves as "a door," meaning that if she is promiscuous and does not show appropriate common sense in the way she deals with men, they will "enclose her with panels of cedar." In this case, they will act as a protective barrier around her in order to prevent others from taking sexual advantage of her. Not just any old planks will be used for this wall, but they will use strong, sturdy and expensive cedar. The use of highly prized cedar panels shows how they care for their sister.

The attitude of these brothers reflects the attitude of their society. They are concerned about their sister's reputation and they look out for her future well-being. Now, God was not only concerned that the women in the Old Testament should remain sexually pure, but he expected sexual purity from both men and women before marriage as well as faithfulness after marriage. In this song God reinforces the message that he has given sexuality as a gift for every couple to enjoy in marriage. Today, God's standards are being undermined in our society and sexual promiscuity is "indulged" through safe sex campaigns. When the institution of marriage is undermined, the ability of people to enjoy a secure love relationship is destroyed. The words of this woman in 8:10 speak about the security she enjoys in her relationship: "I am a wall, and my breasts are like towers. Thus I have become in his eyes like one bringing contentment." By refer- ring to her breasts as towers she disputes her brothers' perception of her level of maturity and she asserts her chastity by saying, "I am a wall." Now that she has become mature and has kept herself sexually pure, she is ready to enter into a marriage relationship with the man she loves and be "like one bringing contentment." She has kept her body pure and now that she is sexually mature, she brings contentment, literally "shalom" or peace, to her husband. Shalom does not only refer to peace in the sense that there is an absence of conflict or fighting, but it involves a much wider sense of fulfillment, satisfaction and blessing. To bring shalom into her husband's life means that she fully satisfies him so that he feels richly blessed because of her. With this wonderful woman in his life he has a feeling of well-being and satisfaction. She is everything that he could ever hope for.

The sense of shalom experienced by this couple is a blessed consequence of the purity that the woman and the man maintained before their marriage. The poet declares that a promiscuous lifestyle is not a foundation on which a young couple can build a strong and satisfying marriage relationship. A promiscuous past undermines the relationship because there is always the sense that someone else has enjoyed the same intimacy with your partner, making shalom in marriage much more challenging to attain. That does not mean it is impossible. When a young man and woman truly repent from their sin and seek to live again according to the pattern given by God, then under God's blessing they can enjoy a good and fruitful marriage. But the things that have happened in the past will always have the ability to challenge the couple's full and complete trust in each other and to undermine the marriage. God's covenant youth who are growing up in this promiscuous society need to take this warning to heart. Being a wall and maintaining your sexual integrity, while not guaranteeing your future happiness, will bring its rewards later in marriage.

Many times I have said that our love for our husband or wife needs to reflect our relationship with Christ, and that is the case in this scenario as well. Sin has destroyed our relationship with God, but Jesus Christ restored that wonderful relationship by his sacrifice on the cross. Christ is the great bridegroom whose love is so great that he bought his bride, the church, with his blood. Now that we have entered into this new relationship with Christ, we need to become a wall against sin in our life and not be like a door allowing it to enter. When the people of Israel became disobedient to God, the Lord accused them of unfaithfulness using the image of an adulterous spouse. His people had run after other lovers. He says, "I gave you wheat and wine and silver and gold and what have you done with all that? You have given it to your lovers. You have run after the gods and idols of this world" (Hosea 2:5–8). From the New Testament perspective, Jesus Christ desires to enter into a faithful and committed relationship with his people. His greatest delight is to enjoy his bride, the church, and to one day present his bride to his Father in heaven as one who is without spot or blemish (Ephesians 5:25–27). For Christ, the greatest shalom and satisfaction is to live with us in a faithful and loving relationship.

An exclusive commitment to the one you love

The words of this song move on in 8:11–12 to a reference to Solomon and one of his vineyards. Solomon was one of the wealthiest kings in Israel and owned many vineyards. This is the only reference in scripture to a vineyard in Baal Hamon, a name which means, "lord of the multitude." The reference to Solomon and his vineyard at this point introduces a new and important element into the song. As verses 11 and 12 indicate, Solomon was unable to personally take care of all his vineyards and, therefore, he rented them out to tenants. The rental price of one thousand pieces of silver for its fruit indicates that this was a prosperous vineyard. The next verse forms a sharp contrast to this when the speaker says, "But my own vineyard is mine to give." It is unclear whether the husband or wife is speaking, but they are very emphatic that their vineyard is their own, in contrast to Solomon who has tenants looking after his vineyard.

In 1:6 of the song, the woman referred to herself as a vineyard, and if we extend that image to this text then this vineyard might refer to a woman as well. But the vineyard in Baal Hamon—lord of the multitude—is one of many that Solomon had, and it could thus also be a reference to the fact that he had many wives. The reference to one thousand pieces of silver may also allude to his many wives, because 1 Kings 11:3 speaks about Solomon's seven hundred wives and three hundred concubines, one thousand in all. If the woman is the speaker in 8:12, then she is boasting about her own independence. Compared to the women in Solomon's harem, she does not need to share the man she loves, but they enjoy each other in an exclusive relationship. On the other hand, if it is the husband who is speaking, then he is boasting about the peace and security of the committed relationship he has with the woman he loves, in contrast to Solomon who has to divide his attention between the many women in his harem.

In the cultural context of the Old Testament, polygamy was often practiced, but the Lord makes clear that he intended the marriage relationship to be monogamous. Love can only flourish in a relationship where there is no competition for that love. The Bible shows how envy and jealousy arose in a number of families where a man had more than one wife. For example, there was trouble between Abraham's wives, Sarah and Hagar, and there was jealousy between Jacob's wives, Rachel and Leah. Love cannot exist in a climate of competition because there will be jealousy, which leads to all sorts of negative behaviour. The Lord Jesus demands the same exclusivity in our relationship with him. Already in the Old Testament the Lord God warned that he would not tolerate his people serving other gods. He warned that in his jealous anger he would punish his people if they betrayed his love by serving other gods and leading a wicked lifestyle. And today, the Lord Jesus will not tolerate it if his bride becomes unfaithful to him. In his jealous love, the Lord Jesus demands our complete and undivided love. There is no room for compromising our commitment to him.

The same is true in our marriage relationships, which cannot tolerate the strain brought on by a spouse who becomes unfaithful. Marriage demands the complete and devoted love of each spouse. It is also important to understand that it is not only other men or women that can compete for our affection. For instance, a husband may substitute his love for his wife with a love of sports, hanging out with friends, pornography or other addictions. Wives can substitute their love for their husbands with a preoccupation with their children, by becoming hooked on social networking or by nurturing other addictions. One can and should have other interests, but these may not take over your marriage relationship. True love means that you are fully committed to your spouse and ready to serve each other out of love, just as Christ expects us to be fully committed to him and ready to serve him out of love.

Desiring the one you love

The husband speaks in 8:13: "You who dwell in the gardens with friends in attendance, let me hear your voice!" It seems rather strange that at the very end of the song, the husband and wife are separated from one another. There are other occasions in the song when they are separated, but they always come together again. At the very end of this song we would expect them to be together, because every good love story ends with the couple living together happily ever after. But that is not the case at the end of this love poem. Instead, he speaks about his beloved dwelling in the gardens where she is with friends in attendance who are listening to her voice. He says, "Let me hear your voice." He is jealous that her companions[2] are able to listen to her voice while he is not able to do so. These words express his longing to be with his wife. In 8:14, the woman in return then takes up an earlier theme with this command to her husband: "Come away [literally, "flee away"], my beloved, and be like a gazelle or like a young stag on the spice-laden mountains." It is not clear whether she means, "flee away from me," or "flee away from something else." But since she expresses a longing to be with her beloved, it is more likely that she wants him to flee away from where he is to the place where she is. She wants him to come to her as quickly as he can.

The expressions the woman uses here remind us of what she said before they were married, when she invited him in 2:17 to come to her "like a gazelle or young stag on the rugged hills." Just as she invited him before they were married, now she again invites him into her garden to enjoy a time of intimacy. On the wedding night, in 4:6, he had responded to her invitation by saying, "Until the day breaks and the shadows flee, I will go to the mountain of myrrh and to the hill of incense." Then they had consummated their marriage and enjoyed a wonderful time of intimacy. But at the end of this song they are separated from each other, even though they still long to be together. This is often the way it is with love and in marriage.

Husbands and wives may be separated from each other for a time by their duties and concerns, each busy with the things of life but always longing to be together. And then this separation is followed by a time in which husband and wife come together again to enjoy a time of intimacy when they can express their love for each other.

Ultimately, this longing of the husband and wife for each other must be a reflection of our relationship with Jesus Christ. The gospel reveals the wonderful love of Jesus Christ, our bridegroom. His love was so great that he laid down his life for us on the cross. There is no greater joy than to experience the love of Christ Jesus. Nothing gives a greater sense of security than to know that our life is safe in the love of Christ who forgives and gives us life everlasting. But there is also a separation in our relationship with Christ, because he has gone to heaven while we are still on this earth. And while on the one hand we fully trust that he is always with us, we still long for the day when our bridegroom will come away from heaven to be with us. It is a mutual longing, because Jesus Christ is working towards that great day when he may present his bride to his Father without any spot or blemish.

The longing that a husband and wife have for each other reflects something of the mystery of our relationship with Jesus Christ. Christ's exclusive relationship with his people must become the foundation on which husband and wife enter into an exclusive marriage relationship. They are so committed to each other that they desire to be faithful to each other through all the circumstances in their lives. True life partners will not let their love grow cold but instead will nourish their love to let it grow and blossom. May the greatest of all love songs be the song that burns in your heart.

For Further Reflection

1. How does the attitude of the brothers reflect the attitude of their society with regard to the reputation of their sister? How does this attitude compare to the attitude in our culture, and should this attitude be reflected in the lives of those who want to follow Jesus Christ?

2. How does the woman's attitude bring shalom (peace) to the marriage relationship? Discuss the concept of shalom and how it is experienced in the relationship.

3. Discuss the woman's assertion that she is a "wall." How does it reflect our relationship with Jesus Christ?

4. How does the reference to Solomon's vineyard at Baal Hamon reflect the desire of the man and woman to have a committed marriage relationship? Compare this to the attitude you have for your marriage.

5. Does this reference to Solomon's vineyard address the practice of polygamy as practiced by Solomon and others in the Old Testament history of Israel? What does it teach about God's intention for marriage?

6. Marriage demands an exclusive relationship of love. Are there things in your marriage that compete for the love of your spouse? Discuss the kinds of changes that you can make.

7. At the end of the song the couple appear separated from each other and there is a longing to be together. Discuss how this reflects the reality of life in a marriage relationship.

8. How does the longing of this couple to be together reflect the longing that God's people have to be with the great bridegroom, Jesus Christ? Discuss how your relationship with Jesus Christ gives you the greatest sense of security and the longing that works in your heart.

9. Discuss how you will keep your love from growing cold and describe how this song of love will continue to burn in your heart.

Works Cited

Bergant, Dianne. "'My Beloved Is Mine and I Am His' (Song 2:16): The Song of Songs and Honor and Shame." *Semeia* 68 (1994): 23–40.

Bergant, Dianne. *The Song of Songs*. Collegeville: Liturgical Press, 2001.

Finch, Karen. "Passover and The Song of Songs." Judaism@suite101, March 14, 2010.

Garrett, Duane. *Song of Songs*. Word Biblical Commentary, vol. 23B. Waco: Word Books, 2004.

Gledhill, Tom. *The Message of the Song of Songs*. Downers Grove: Inter-Varsity Press, 1994.

Harris, R. Laird, Gleason L. Archer and Bruce K. Waltke. *Theological Wordbook of the Old Testament*, vol. 2. Chicago: Moody, 1980.

Heidelberg Catechism. *Book of Praise: Anglo-Genevan Psalter*. Winnipeg: Premier Printing, 2014.

Hess, Richard S. *Song of Songs*. Grand Rapids: Baker Academic, 2005.

Jeffrey, David L., ed. *A Dictionary of Biblical Tradition in English Literature*. Grand Rapids: Eerdmans, 1992.

Keel, Othmar. *The Song of Songs: A Continental Commentary*. Minneapolis: Fortress Press, 1994.

Longman, Tremper, III. *Song of Songs*. New International Commentary on the Old Testament. Grand Rapids: Eerdmans, 2001.

Lundbom, J.R. "Song of Songs 3:1–4." *Interpretation* 49, No. 2 (1995): 172–175.

Nelson, Tommy. *The Book of Romance: What Solomon Says About Love, Sex, and Intimacy*. Nashville: Thomas Nelson, 1998.

Parrott, Les and Leslie. *Saving Your Marriage Before It Starts*. Grand Rapids: Zondervan, 1995.

Pope, Marvin H. *Song of Songs*. The Anchor Bible. Garden City: Doubleday, 1977.

Provan, Iain. *Ecclesiastes, Song of Songs*. The NIV Application Commentary. Grand Rapids: Zondervan, 2001.

Williamson, G. I. *The Song of Songs: A Series of Sermons on the Song of Solomon*. Published by the author, 1981.

End Notes

Introduction

1. Included in the wisdom literature are Job, some Psalms, Proverbs, Ecclesiastes and Song of Songs.
2. If this is a collection of love songs, then originally many of the songs may have been written with a specific couple in mind, but once the poems were placed together in a collection the editor created a fictional couple demonstrating what every couple in Israel strives for in their relationship.
3. For an excellent introduction to the Song of Songs that interacts with many of the discussions around this song see Tremper Longman III, *The Song of Songs* (NICOT: Grand Rapids: Eerdmans Publishing, 2001).

Chapter 1

1. See what scripture says about the insatiable appetite of lust: Proverbs 30:15–16; Ephesians 4:19.
2. Diane Bergant argues that the woman in the Song of Songs appears to be an "unorthodox character" as she breaks the mould of the typical role played by women in her culture. (See "Song of Songs and Honor and Shame.")
3. The headship of the man over his wife is an important concept in scripture. In 1 Timothy 2:11–14, Paul shows that the concept of

headship began with Adam and Eve, and in Ephesians 5:23–25 he argues that the headship of the man over his wife is patterned after the headship of Jesus Christ. The Song of Songs reveals God's intention for the way husbands and wives are to relate to each other in the roles that the Lord gives them in marriage.

4. Scripture refers to the church of Christ as the bride of Christ. Therefore, in our relationship with Christ we look to him as our bridegroom, and he looks to us as his bride. (See Ephesians 5:23–30; Revelation 19:7; 21:1, 9.)

Chapter 2

1. In Genesis 25:13 and 1 Chronicles 1:29 Kedar is listed among the descendants of Ishmael. They were a powerful Bedouin tribe in northern Arabia from the 8th to the 4th century BC.

2. If it is the young man who speaks, he pays her a wonderful compliment by calling her the "most beautiful of women." On the other hand the daughters of Jerusalem or the editor of the song might also observe the wonderful character of this girl and describe her with these glowing words. In the end the interpretation of the text does not depend on determining who gives the advice.

Chapter 3

1. In 1:8 there is an interjection by someone who gives advice to the woman. While some suggest it is the beloved who speaks there, it is more likely that this advice comes from another source.

2. In Deuteronomy 17:16 Moses forbade any future king in Israel from acquiring great numbers of horses.

3. 1 Kings 4:26: "Solomon had four thousand stalls for chariot horses, and twelve thousand horses."

4. The Heidelberg Catechism asks in Lord's Day 45, "Why is prayer necessary for Christians?" It answers, "Because prayer is the most important part of the thankfulness which God requires of us." Paul commands in 1 Thessalonians 5:17–18,

"Pray continually; give thanks in all circumstances, for this is God's will for you in Christ Jesus." He also gives this encouragement in Ephesians 5:20, "always giving thanks to God the Father for everything, in the name of our Lord Jesus Christ."

5. Pictures of this beautiful oasis can be found by doing an Internet search for "En Gedi."

Chapter 4

1. It should be understood that although the NIV translates "a rose of Sharon," it is impossible for this to be a modern rose as they were not introduced to Israel until after the Old Testament period. The only other mention of this flower in the Old Testament is found in Isaiah 35:1–2 where the NIV translates it as a "crocus." In that context, the barren desert will burst forth into blossom: "Like the crocus it will burst into bloom." The blooming of this flower in the desert is compared to the glory of Lebanon and the splendour of Carmel and Sharon.
As to the "lily of the valleys," the same word is used to describe the flower with which Solomon decorated the glorious temple of God. The top of the pillars in the portico of the temple were made in the shape of lilies (1 Kings 7:19, 22). In the temple there was also the Sea, a great water basin with a rim like a lily blossom (1 Kings 7:26). This lily is used by Solomon to decorate the glorious house of God.

2. The woman uses both the rose and the lily to describe herself. When we compare how the rose and lily are used in scripture, it becomes difficult to maintain that the woman is being self-deprecating, although that may be an appealing interpretation, especially in contrast to the man's elevation of her in the next verse by saying that she is like a "lily among thorns"; in other words, she is not just a mere flower but something special in comparison to others. On the other hand, we can also understand his words to mean that while the woman confidently compares herself to a rose of Sharon or a lily of the valleys, he regards her as a lily among thorns when compared to other women. In other words, she is the only flower that holds

any interest for him since she is the most beautiful woman in his eyes.

3. The only other place the word "banner" is used in scripture is in the book of Numbers where the people of Israel camp or walk under the standard, or banner, of their tribe. A standard identified each tribe of Israel. (See Numbers 1:52; 2:2, 17, 31, 34.)

4. Literally the text says, "He has taken me to the house of wine," which the NIV has translated as the "banquet hall." While this is the only use of this phrase in scripture, Longman points to near synonyms in Esther 7:8, "house for the drinking of wine," as well as Jeremiah 16:8 and Ecclesiastes 7:2, which speak about the "drinking house" (112). These references refer to definite places where people would meet to enjoy a good time, perhaps to enjoy a banquet or feast where they would drink wine. The woman says that the one she loves takes her to "the house of wine." The definite article indicates that this was a specific place where people would meet and wine was drunk.

5. One of the difficulties in interpreting the song is to understand where to draw certain lines. In this context, the passion between the man and woman runs very high and therefore it is easy to conclude as some do that the embrace must describe a sexual encounter. When we examine the use of the verb "embrace" in scripture it is used for the affectionate embrace of a son by a father (Genesis 48:10), and it is also used to refer to a man's sexual grasp of the bosom of an adulterous woman (Proverbs 5:20). The embrace described in this song is a passionate embrace of a man and woman who love one another, but we cannot conclude from this that the woman is speaking about a sexual encounter especially in light of her next words, in 2:7.

6. See Longman 115; NIV footnote on 2:7.

Chapter 7

1. Commentators have variously attributed these words to the man or the woman in the song. Others argue that the editor added the words, and still others that they are an independent poem inserted at this point.

2. Because 3:6–11 does not describe the relationship between the man and woman but rather the splendour of Solomon's litter, it is difficult to connect it to the broader text of the song. Longman writes, "It is Solomon's wealth and grandeur that are being applied to emphasize the magnificence of the wedding and, by association, the marriage relationship itself" (136).
3. Saul was the first king in Israel but David's family became the royal family. Solomon had many wives as a result of alliances he made with foreign rulers and these must have been lavish weddings.
4. *National Post*, week of Dec. 1, 2009.
5. These women are skilled at what they do but the emphasis is on the fact that they do this work with great love. These women of Jerusalem are motivated by a deep affection for the king as they work on the interior of his carriage.
6. See Exodus 23:16, Leviticus 27:30–32, 1 Corinthians 16:1–3.

Chapter 8

1. It is also possible to argue that he only mentions seven features of her body, if her lips and mouth are understood to refer to the same feature. (See Longman 145.)
2. The sheep's wool becomes dirty over time, but when the sheep are shorn they appear clean and white again. Therefore, the whiteness of this woman's teeth is compared to that of freshly shorn sheep.
3. Compare this to what the Preacher says about the elderly in Ecclesiastes 12:3: "the grinders cease because they are few."
4. Some other conjectures as to the meaning of the Hebrew word are "weapon" or "layers, courses" which would indicate a tower that is build up with layers of stone.

Chapter 9

1. Keel explains, "It is a metaphor, meant to express the intense feeling of relatedness and solidarity that has animated lovers in every age" (163). See Genesis 2:23, 2 Samuel 19:12–13.

2. The Septuagint, the Greek translation of the Old Testament, uses "paradise" as a translation of the Hebrew word "orchard." In the mind of the ancient reader this would clearly have been an allusion to paradise in Genesis 2:8. (See Harris 733: park, enclosed garden.)

Chapter 10

1. Keel refers to a poem of Lucretius from the first century BC in which the lover is shut out by the woman he loves. He covers the threshold with flowers and anoints the doorposts with oil to leave behind a message of his love (194).

Chapter 11

1. The woman refers to herself as "his" garden for she has completely given herself to him.
2. The covenant child who seeks the Lord in faith knows where God can be found because the Lord is faithful to his promise.

Chapter 12

1. I am indebted to G. I. Williamson for this perspective (56).
2. Paul writes to the Philippians about the role that Jesus has as the Saviour. He writes that everyone who confesses Jesus as Lord will be saved, "to the glory of God the Father" (Philippians 2:11).
3. In this song the Lord deals with the roles husbands and wives are called to fulfill in their marriage relationship. We should keep in mind that they also have another role as parents. The book of Proverbs is more directed to the role of parents for there wisdom is personified as a father giving instruction to his son.
4. There is much discussion among scholars whether verses 11–12 are spoken by the man or the woman. The Hebrew text does not give any indication, so the choice is really determined by one's interpretation of this text.

5. In Ezekiel 16 we find an allegory in which Jerusalem is compared to a girl who is rescued by God, who then enters into a marriage bond with her. In the prophecy of Hosea, the Lord accuses Israel of becoming unfaithful to him as a wife becomes unfaithful to her husband. In both Ezekiel and Hosea, the Lord God is the faithful bridegroom who has to deal with an unfaithful bride.
6. See the warning against the adulteress in Proverbs 5 and 7 and her destruction in Revelation 17 and 18.

Chapter 13

1. We are dealing with the last part of a larger section in the song. The larger section includes 3:6–8:4 and is framed by the refrain, "Daughters of Jerusalem, I charge you" (3:5 and 8:5). The words in 7:1–8:3 are a single unit, and the words of the woman in 7:10, "I belong to my beloved, and his desire is for me," stand in the centre of that unit giving us a window into understanding this part of the song.

Chapter 14

1. See Proverbs 5:15–18, where a man is commanded to drink from his own cistern, rejoicing in the wife of his youth.

Chapter 15

1. Romans 4:11: "And he [Abraham] received the sign of circumcision, a seal of the righteousness he had by faith while he was still uncircumcised."
2. Jesus once told the parable about the Pharisee and the tax collector. The Pharisee boasted about all the things he had done for God and thought he had earned God's love, but the tax collector beat his breast in humility and said, "God, have mercy on me, a sinner." Jesus said that the man who humbled himself will be justified—that is, saved. God's love is freely given and cannot be bought or earned (Luke 18:10–14).

Chapter 16

1. Every generation speaks about living in the "last days" as they await the return of Jesus Christ.
2. The Hebrew indicates that these companions were males, but it is difficult to determine whether there is a specific reason why they are male companions.